M000012650

Tr[aveler's]

to

Monumental Treasures

in the U.S.A.

Museums - Monuments - Mansions

by Hal Thornton

Legacy Press
Santa Barbara, California

TRAVELER'S GUIDE TO MONUMENTAL TREASURES IN THE U.S.A.

Copyright 1990 by Hal Thornton

All rights reserved. No part of this book may be reproduced in any form or by any electronic or mechanical means including information storage and retrieval systems without permission in writing from the publisher, except by a reviewer who may quote brief passages in a review.

Although the author and publisher have used reasonable diligence to ensure the accuracy and completeness of this book, we assume no responsibility for inaccuracies, errors, omissions or inconsistency herein. Readers should contact the site for current information. Editorial opinion infiltrates throughout.

Published by:
Legacy Press
32 West Anapamu St., Suite 284
Santa Barbara, CA 93101

Printed and bound in U.S.A. First Edition.
Printing 10 9 8 7 6 5 4 3 2 1

Library of Congress Cataloging-in-Publication Data 90-61808

Thornton, Hal
Traveler's Guide to Monumental Treasures in the United States

Includes index.
1. Guide to mansions, monuments, and museums
2. Biographical sketch of creators
3. Historical perspective of creation
4. Data and recommendations on how to visit
5. Names and Addresses of non-profit organizations

ISBN 0-9627114-3-8   (Softcover): $15.95

Cover design by Robert Howard
Typography by Keith Messinger, *ScanDo!*

Front cover photo credits top to bottom, left to right:
Mount Rushmore, photo courtesy of Mount Rushmore National Monument; Hearst Castle, photo courtesy of Hearst San Simeon State Historical Monument; Vizcaya, photo courtesy of Vizcaya Museum and Gardens; Nemours garden, photo courtesy of Nemours Museum and Gardens; Stan Hywet Hall, photo courtesy of Stan Hywet Hall Foundation, Inc.; Hotel del Coronado, photo courtesy of Hotel del Coronado.

Back cover photo credits left to right:
San Sylmar interior, photo courtesy of Merle Norman Cosmetics; Newport Breakers, photo courtesy of the Preservation Society of Newport County.

Dedication

to Jeanne. My travel companion for half a century.
Ever willing despite motion sickness, altered
plans and strange languages.

Ever ready despite a preference to be snug
at home with her flower garden and near
to our grandkids.

Table of Contents

iv

CALIFORNIA COAST

The above commercial accommodations have been included because they should be unique extensions of the experience. They are travel destinations on their own merit; they are extraordinary; they relate to the era and aura of the attractions to which they are proximate.

Acknowledgement

To the HOSTS . . . a TOAST!

Many, many thanks to the unsung. Those who have made the
attractions in this book come alive . . .
VOLUNTEERS   DOCENTS   GUIDES
ESCORTS   INTERPRETERS   "PR-PERSONS"
AUXILIARIES   FRIENDS OF THE . . .
FUND RAISERS
By whatever name they are known, they are part of the
great legacies. They too are our benefactors.
Just as the creators of these monuments have bequeathed
to the public untold wealth, those who devote
their time and talent to preserve the
memory and magnify it . . .
they too are philanthropists.
Be they unpaid or underpaid, their devotion is a gift
of love.
And how do we thank the fund raisers and the contributors
of the money to restore and keep operating so that
these sight-seeing opportunities may stay
open to the public? They wouldn't do
it if their heart weren't in it.
And of course, the experts in the Tour and Travel industry
who take care of the pesky arrangements . . . I hereby appoint
you HONORARY DOCENTS.
A salute to all of you. HOW I WISH I COULD NAME YOU
EACH AND EVERY ONE!

More Acknowledgements
. . . from the author

Thanks to others, my rambling opinions in file folders may in time become astute observations because they are now between covers.

My three daughters and Jo assured me I *could* write it.
My travel agents, the Emrichs, told me I *should* write it.
My wife plied me with nutrients to ensure that I *would* write it.

Credit is due Kay Strom, Nancy Gibson and Marjorie Shore (for critiquing) . . . Mary Nosker's word processing went far beyond mere disc-feeding . . . Keith Messinger (at ScanDo!) scan-did the typesetting . . . There were plug-ins from Cork, Dan and Anne, Lindse and Linda, Anna (my gorgeous postmistress) and Courtney . . . Joseph Makray drew my likeness . . . Robert Howard did the cover.

"Senior Coupons" have made Delta my favorite airline.

Luckily, I have some friends with historical insight, including (but not limited to) Maurice Hudkins (a memory bank for great achievers, whether east or west) and Mort and Penn Borden (students of Jefferson and Roosevelt).

Three sons-in-law participated (unknowingly) because my grandkids (there are several) sneak into my story. They challenge me with their smarts, and I lean on them for help with chores. Kate and Kirsten tell me I am an awesome dude. It's a distinction I struggle to validate.

This book is about traveling, but coming home is the flip-side of tripping and just as pleasurable, thanks to my tennis and bridge partners; the folks with Adult-Ed and City College; to Unitarians and Rotarians; and sundry other friends who I hope will, for many years to come, welcome me home!

I'm Into Rare Art and Trophy Properties . . . .

Up the coast a bit, I have a castle loaded with baubles that would make kings and queens covetous. This property was willed to me by the Hearst family. They even made a deal with the State of California to take care of it. The Parks Department does a terrific job.

Much of my art is stashed down the coast, in my Roman villa at Herculaneum. I inherited it from John Paul Getty. He never saw it, poor guy, but he thoughtfully arranged to have it protected and tended. J. Paul even provided undercover parking. I really appreciate that.

Getty and the Hearst family wanted these treasures to be shared by the public. That's how I struck it rich. If it's public domain, my name is on the deed—as is everyone else's. My co-owners are legion. They're rich and poor, camera-toters and note-takers, Asians, Africans and Australians, Latinos and Europeans; Canadians, too. All are welcome. The more the merrier.

This is only a part of my vast holdings. However, my portfolio has value only to the extent to which I seek it out and enjoy it. If California slides into the ocean, some of my best properties will be lost. If the ice cap melts, Vizcaya and my Ringling art treasures in Florida are goners. But Mount Rushmore will still be high and dry. The Carnegie at Pittsburgh is safely inland. My legacies are well dispersed across the nation and are in good management hands. Someone is paying the bills, I guess, because I never see them.

Whitehall — Courtesy Henry M. Flagler Museum

Whitehall

Mr. Florida - Mr. Right! - and his Granddaughter
Quite "a little bit of bloomin' luck . . . "

Henry Morrison Flagler did a lot of things right. A preacher's kid, born in 1830, he left his home in New York State to rise above the poverty line. Found a job in a relative's store in Ohio. Earned five dollars a month. Worked hard, saved his money, had a good business head. Just your typical teenager. And just the sort of fellow Mary Harkness, the boss's daughter, wanted to marry.

A good wholesome TV sitcom circa 1853: Middle America, mid-century. Promising, God-fearing yuppie couple with three children. Upwardly mobile Henry buys into in-law's company, helps it prosper, sells out, goes into salt production business on his own. Salt's good until the Civil War ends, then bankruptcy. Borrows $40,000 to pay debts, moves to the big city (Cleveland), goes into grain business, meets kindred spirit with same entrepreneurial itch. New friend's name? John D. Rockefeller. From here on, all their troubles will be big ones. Like their dividends.

By age forty Henry Flagler is Secretary-Treasurer of Standard Oil Company. With a bit of imagination one can figure he's "in the money". The "John and Henry" show makes so much money they both take up philanthropy as a full-time occupation. John gives away dimes and/or millions; Henry's favorite charity is Florida—a somewhat pestilential swampland which needs a railroad to open it up.

Florida! As history goes, about the year 1513, Ponce de Leon heard there was g-o-l-d in Florida, and he set off to find it. The native Seminoles, who had heard bad rumors about the Spaniards, drilled Ponce with an arrow and sent him home bled white. Ponce de Leon was the first in a long parade of gold seekers. What he didn't know then was that FLORIDA gold had to be brought down by escapees from the northern winters who would pay dearly for deeds to underwater lots. Ponce was four hundred years too early.

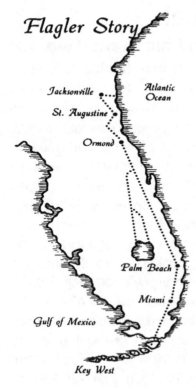

Flagler Story

Jacksonville
St. Augustine
Ormond
Atlantic Ocean
Palm Beach
Miami
Gulf of Mexico
Key West

Map courtesy of
Henry M. Flagler Museum.

For the next three hundred years, ownership of Florida was tossed around like a trading chip among the European superpowers. In 1821 our Congress decided to get into the game with a $5 million ante. This took Florida off the market. Also made President Jackson very happy; someday there'd be a Florida town named for him. On the other hand, it made the Seminole natives very unhappy because they already knew from experience that Andrew Jackson didn't like them. The Seminoles were a pretty decent tribe who thought they were where God wanted them and couldn't care less about the claims to their land by the foreigners.

Over the years, it cost the U.S. $40 million in military action to convince the Seminoles they were wrong. By now the U.S. was into Florida land some $45 million, which was way too much, and it set a trend. For the next seventy years not much happened, pending the arrival of Ponce de Leon II—aka James Flagler.

By 1883, Mary Flagler's health was failing. The couple tried Jacksonville (end of the rail line) for a better climate, but it wasn't the answer. Mary died, ending twenty-eight years of good married life. Two years later, Flagler married the nurse who had attended his wife's illness. Back to Florida he went for a honeymoon—St. Augustine this time. Flagler was getting hooked on Florida and the die was cast.

Evidently Flagler looked into the future, realized that someday frost-bitten northerners would scramble to Florida with their money and would need a way to get there. Once there was a time Americans travelled by train. Especially rich Americans. And rich travelers needed deluxe hotel accommodations. Someone must build trendy hotels. Railroads and Hotels! Flagler found his second career.

Florida consumed the remainder of Henry's life. He built the Ponce de Leon at St. Augustine (now Flagler College), the Cordova, the Alcazar, the Ormond, and the Royal Poinciana at Palm Beach. When the latter opened in 1894, it was the largest wooden hotel in the world, and claimed to be the country's most fashionable (a boast the Del Coronado, on the opposite coast, would most certainly dispute). Less pretentious was the Palm Beach Inn, which in time was enlarged and renamed The Breakers. This was destroyed by fire in 1903, rebuilt and enlarged, and in 1925 was again rebuilt even larger—this time by Flagler heirs (see its story on page 8).

The Flagler railroad strategy was to buy up small trackages in order to connect the northeast states to Florida without train transfers. His Florida East Coast Railroad kept pace with the hotels, and in time Mr. Flagler's private rail car was parked at Worth Lake, looking across to Palm Beach.

Palm Beach was deep enough into creepy-crawly country to satisfy most of the sun seekers. But further down the sandy strand, a wily widow was staring at her section of worthless waterfront next to a fort named Dallas. If there was one thing that would redeem her bad buy, it was a railroad. Julia D. Tuttle waved land at Flagler. It was an offer he couldn't refuse. What resulted from this chicanery should be called Flaglerville-Tuttle City. But for some odd reason Flagler chose to use the Indian name, Miami.

Flagler and Tuttle may have been opportunists, but they were not mean. They couldn't possibly have foreseen themselves as progenitors to an impossible-to-manage megalopolis.

All was not wine and roses in this success story. The death of Mary Harkness may have confounded Flagler's good judgment, for his second marriage to Ida Alice Shrouds was wrong for the Flagler script. Their time together was short, and most of Ida Alice's remaining years were spent in an asylum. Flagler divorced her after ensuring she would have the best of care. He endowed a trust for her. She outlived the rest of the family and died wealthy. During this time of emotional turbulence, Henry's beloved daughter died just weeks after she had given birth to, and lost, a baby girl. Flagler knew loneliness. He had been into the valley of sorrow. His sitcom had pathos.

Then came a new century, a new wife, and with her a new lifestyle. In a new house. Well, not really a house. More like a European palace! Mary Lily Kenan was just right for Flagler. They were married in August of 1901. She was a charming beauty at thirty-four. He was seventy-one. It was a good match. For a wedding present she asked for the moon. Flagler wanted her to have it and with some stars thrown in. His present was named "Whitehall."

It would take a sizable book to describe the wonders of Whitehall. It is what a southern belle would design if she knew her generous husband would have $100 million left, no matter what she spent.

The major rooms were decorated in historic European styles. The huge entrance hall, 110 feet long and 40 wide, suggests the atrium of a Roman villa covered by a baroque ceiling like those of Louis XIV's Versailles. Part of the design was by the noted firm, Carrere & Hastings. Other interiors were by the New York firm, Pottier and Stymus.

The opulent music room reflects the talents of Mary Lily Flagler. An accomplished singer, she had a resident organist employed for each season. I was entranced by a recessed dome in the ceiling, illuminated by hidden light bulbs. It seemed an unusual refinement for 1901. The room has two massive French chandeliers of gilt bronze and Baccarat crystal.

The ballroom! Ah-h-h! A musician's balcony, gilded mirrors, gilded benches, Rose du Barry silk damask draperies, soft lights reflecting off a polished floor! What excitement the guests must have experienced many years later when the Restoration Ball marked the re-opening of this showplace in February of 1960.

By the early 1900s, Flagler had pushed his railroad to the end of the route. Florida stretched no further. His private car, "The Rambler" (F.E.C. #90), had carried him to Key West, the outer reach of his railroading days. It was January 1912. He exulted with his own benediction: "My dream is fulfilled . . . now I can die happy." Sixteen months later, he was dead.

What of the monument? He did not give Whitehall to the public. It belonged to Mary Lily. She left it to her niece, Louise Clisby Wise, who sold it to developers. They added a hotel, which in time succumbed to age. Both Whitehall and its hotel appendage might have been razed—except for Jean Flagler Mathews.

In the great marble hall is Jean Flagler Mathews' full-length portrait. Henry Flagler never saw this beautiful lady. He could only have seen her as an infant, the baby daughter of his son, Harry Harkness! Yet her presence permeates Whitehall, as it should. She saved it for all of us. She was a special person.

Even though this exciting collection of art and architecture attests to the taste of Mary Lily and reflects the stature of Henry Flagler, it is a public legacy because of Jean Flagler Mathews. She knew Whitehall symbolized her grandfather. She recognized an irreplaceable treasure. She spearheaded the foundation that bought it, restored it and opened it to the public.

For nineteen years Jean Flagler Mathews presided over the great events at Whitehall, and at each anniversay's open house she personally greeted the guests. She did this until her death in 1979, at the age of sixty-eight.

She was equally active in her home in Rye, New York, where she was an ardent horticulturist and a member of the Botanical Gardens. She was a graduate of the Chapin School in Manhattan and held an honorary doctorate from the University of the South at Sewanee, Tennessee.

If Whitehall could speak, might it not warn us that a monument of this calibre must ultimately belong to the public? That the arrangement should be made while the owners are still of sound mind and body? Failing that, do pray for a child or grandchild with heart and vision and resources.

Of course, in a broader sense, all of Florida is a Flagler monument. But how many know that? Do the millions who crowd the beaches and the Space Center and EPCOT and the Orlando Carnival know they're in Flaglerland? And who now needs railroads? But Whitehall is there to remind us that, for one brief, shining twelve-year moment, Palm Beach had its Camelot.

The Breakers (Hotel)
A Very Palm Beach Tradition

Henry Morrison Flagler, railroad magnate and co-founder of the Standard Oil Company with John D. Rockefeller, is credited with fathering development of the east coast of Florida. In transforming this area into a vacationland for millions of people, he built the Palm Beach Inn in 1895. The Inn proved so successful it was enlarged three times by 1901. In 1903 it was completely destroyed by fire, but was immediately replaced with a finer, more commodious structure and renamed The Breakers.

Back then, guests came to Palm Beach on Flagler's railroad, and private railroad cars parked behind what is now the Post Office at the end of Royal Poinciana Way. From there, arriving guests rode by a donkey-drawn surrey along the Pine Walk (now the Beach Club entrance) to the Breakers.

The tradition of elegant charity balls, which attracted society leaders and celebrities the world over, has continued through the years. Many gala events mark each "season," including New Year's Eve, and George Washington and St. Patrick's Day Balls.

The Breaker's cottages, which originally lined the beach- front on both sides of the hotel, were reserved in that era as winter homes by prominent families. Some of these early guests were John D. Rockefeller, John Jacob Astor, J. P. Morgan, President Warren C.

Harding, William Randolph Hearst, the Duchess of Marlborough (Consuelo Vanderbilt) and Andrew Carnegie.

Flagler's third marriage to Mary Lily Kenan in 1901 certainly gilded his lifestyle for his remaining twelve years. And Mary Lily had the good luck to have two brothers capable of picking up the Flagler System reins. William Kenan, and then Frank, became the key managers of Flagler money, part of which now flows through the Kenan Charitable Trust. When the second wooden Breakers burned in 1925, William Kenan decided on a permanent, impressive replacement worthy of the Flagler tradition. It was Kenan's dream to make The Breakers the finest resort hotel in the world, a fitting tribute to Henry Morrison Flagler who had made Palm Beach a resort of international acclaim.

William Kenan commissioned architect Leonard Schultze, well-known for his design of the Waldorf-Astoria, to design the hotel. Schultze declared the site so magnificent it was worthy of nothing less than an Italian palace. Guided by this inspiration, he drew up plans for a resort hotel fashioned after the most outstanding structures in Italy. Some 1200 craftsmen worked shifts around the clock to meet the opening date. Seventy-five artists from Italy were engaged to create the magnificent frescoes on the ceilings.

On December 29, 1926, The Breakers re-opened its doors as one of the most splendid architectural and artistic achievements of its era. More than $6,000,000 was spent to create this majestic resort hotel in a record-breaking twelve months, on what many feel is the most commanding site on the eastern seacoast. Architectural journals called it the finest resort hotel in America—and considering that its cost was more than the U.S. paid for all of Florida in 1821, who's surprised?

The exterior of the hotel, with its twin belvedere towers and graceful arches, was inspired by the famous Villa Medici in Florence. The Florentine fountain in front of the hotel is patterned after the one in the Bobli Gardens in Florence. The decor of its public rooms reflects the artistry of the Italian Renaissance. Several fine 15th-century Flemish tapestries grace the walls. The lobby, with its frescoed,

The Breakers Hotel — Palm Beach Florida

vaulted ceiling, captures the essence of the Palazzo Carega in Genoa, and overlooks a colorful central courtyard similar to the inner gardens of the Villa Sante in Rome. This tranquil courtyard is bordered by loggias leading eastward toward the blue Atlantic. At the ocean end of the courtyard stands the Mediterranean Ballroom, inspired by the Palazzo Deg'l Imperial at Genoa. The ceiling in the Gold Room is an exact duplicate of the ceiling in the Galleria Accademia on the Grand Canal in Venice. Portraits of Renaissance rulers and explorers who participated in the discovery and development of the New World surround the Gold Room. The overpanel of the great Stone Fireplace depicts the New World emerging from the clouds of the Old World.

Then there is the circle dining room. Here I savored a picture-perfect room. Breakfast was served on a richly-colored cloth, tableware glistened, and overhead soared a domed ceiling painted with murals of Italian cities. From the center sparkled an exquisite chandelier of bronze and mirrors and crystal. It captivated me. The waitress told me the chandelier was Venetian. "How about the nifty little Chambord France jelly jars? Might I take them to my wife as a consolation?"

The waitress looked "why?" at me.

"She couldn't make this event. It would mean something special if I brought her a remembrance from Europe . . . "

"Wait—I'll get you an extra . . . ," she smiled as she dashed away.

I looked at my tab. Only $15.00. Hmm . . . I've saved round-trip fare to Venice plus water taxi to the Hotel Danieli. It's savings enough to fly Jeanne here for the weekend. Why not! The Kenans would be pleased; so would our travel agents.

Photo courtesy of Vizcaya Museum and Garden, Miami, Florida

Vizcaya
A Montage

. . . In northern Spain the shores are washed by the Bay of Biscay. In southern Florida, Biscayne Bay washes the shore where Vizcaya basques . . . and as if by magic two continents are joined . . .

Do you have the Venice itch? Do you dream of being delivered to your palace door by a costumed gondolier? Does your dream have the sound of sea water lapping at a bulwark ringed with painted gondola poles? Lucky you. For a reasonable facsimile is yours with easy travel arrangements. No interminable droning through the night at 40,000 feet while you want to stretch out and can't, no currency scramble, no over-priced boatman.

The feel of Venice, and for less than ten thousand lira, is as easy as (1) departing your car or taxi at Haulover Beach Park (Collins & 108th Street), Miami Beach, (2) boarding a comfortable sightseeing boat to shuttle you to your Venetian Holiday, and (3) letting your imagination loose!

As your boat nears the sea wall you float into an era gone by, to the fortress-like Villa Rezzonico at Bassana del Grappa in the Italian Veneto. As your boatman ties up to the sea wall, marvel at the great stone barge which acts as a breakwater, then step ashore through a tea house, walk over a quaint canal bridge and mount the broad steps to the Villa. Pay a token cover charge to the doorkeeper, and presto—you are one rich legatee!

This villa, with its seventy rooms that required a staff of thirty, was the winter home for Mr. James Deering, and for only eight winters. James was a son of William Deering, who developed the Deering harvester machine. In 1902 the firm merged with McCormick

Harvester and other companies to form the International Harvester Company, of which James Deering was vice president.

For many years, in addition to his Chicago home, Deering maintained a residence in France, which helps explain his love for the matchless art treasures brought to Vizcaya.

The European revival took four hundred years to span the periods that have been labeled Renaissance, Baroque, Rococo and Neoclassic. And yet, along the shores of Biscayne Bay the visitor has a montage instantly under one roof. All it required was James Deering's money and a skilled designer with lots of vision. Plus 180 acres of pinewood brush land in the heart of Miami-to-be.

"Vizcaya is pure theatre," wrote Carl J. Weinhardt (fourth Director): "Paul Chalfin (the designer) would have been a superb theatrical designer. Every room in Vizcaya is a 'set,' the kind that used to cause a gasp of delight and spontaneous applause when the curtain went up on the first act the opening night of a new play. So, ladies and gentlemen, you're on stage!"

Indeed! James Deering's monument transplanted the romance of Venice to our own continent. For this he chose three young stars who must share the applause: Paul Chalfin, the designer who travelled with Deering throughout Europe; F. Burrall Hoffman, an architect with the right mentors; and Diego Suarez, landscape architect trained in Italy, whose work continued long after completion of the structure.

Imagine! Here you are, in an earlier hangout for U.S. presidents, captains of industry, rank and nobility. Among the guests: Rose Reilly Douras tending her adolescent cutup, who would catch the attention of another notable guest, William Randolph Hearst. This random encounter with starlet Marion Davies blossomed into a liaison that filled box offices and party rosters for forty years to come.

The human drama here may have had mystic influence from carvings in the entry which were more than mere art. The marble statue of Bacchus, god of wine and revelry, seems to preside over a carved Roman basin, but a far more sinister revelry was perceived by my imaginative guide who suspected that Bacchus and Dionysus were a party to the first beauty contest, where Paris, mortal-man-appointed-judge, explained to three goddesses that he could be more objective if they disrobed. It turned, of course, into a contest of lies and bribery aimed at winning the Golden Apple. An unguided stroller might think these were just decorations. Nonsense!

Never pass up the advantages that guides and docents can offer. That's why they are there. At Vizcaya, I daresay I was better briefed because of my guide than President Reagan and Pope John Paul II when they met for a photo-op in the Renaissance Hall in September of 1987. What did they discuss? These walls hold a lot of secrets.

Deering suffered from pernicious anemia, a disease for which doctors of that era could do little more than advise a warm winter climate. In 1912 he purchased the land which now sites the fabulous creation: Vizcaya.

Deering was born in Paris (Maine—11/12/1859); he died aboard Paris (the S.S.—9/21/1925) while crossing the Atlantic. He never married, and Vizcaya passed to his nieces. For them it must have been a nagging perplexity—how to sustain a complex creation that was bigger than life. In private hands, its size was its Achilles heel. In 1952 the owners and the Dade County Commissioners initiated a rescue plan. "Vizcayans" and volunteer guides joined the challenge. We, the public, are indebted to a host of dedicated and generous donors who rescued Vizcaya and now sustain it.

I have a kinship with Vizcaya that intensifies my personal gratitude. It is haunting. In a way we are twins. Well, nearly. I was born the same week James Deering first occupied his Villa, Christmas 1916. So together, though a continent apart, Vizcaya and I have aged. We have felt the toll of time and the elements, Vizcaya from tropical heat and salt air decay, and I from the Arctic cold. Late, but not fatally so, Vizcaya received climate control (1987); and late, but not fatally so, I escaped to the moderate breezes of Santa Barbara. There the affinity could end, for what was the slim chance that the son of a minister to a rural Kansas church would ever walk the halls of this opulent palace?

And yet, there is this lucky happenstance, like the stories we hear of separate twins who finally find each other. Although they bemoan the lost years, they value the time remaining so much more. There is a euphoria in the discovery of a delight of which we knew nothing. This book is intended to lead the reader to over forty legacies, treasures in the public domain—but treasures only if they are claimed, enjoyed only if viewed and embraced.

"What is Vizcaya but deja vu on a grand scale? A stage set, real and unreal, a glamorous assemblage of what was once the American dream. It is a state of mind now an anachronism, an historical moment, the exquisite expression of an age caught in amber—so much better than it has any right to be . . . "

- Carl Weinhardt

Photo courtesy of Biltmore Hotel, Coral Gables, Florida

The Biltmore
A Hotel With Niŋe Lives

This Phoenix risen from its ashes, this gemstone of Miami, this magnificent monument—a survivor, snatched from the brink—has roller-coastered along the precipice for more than sixty years and is again alive and well.

Maybe this story can be better understood as a TV sitcom. Here's the outline: A Congregational preacher named Solomon Merrick wants to escape from New England winters. He is conned into sinking the family nest egg, all $1,100, into 160 acres of worthless pineland in the Florida boonies. It's the 1890s, about sixty years before air conditioning will be in vogue.

Year 1899: The family migrates to the promised land . . . which it isn't. They brave yellow fever, snakes, rats, jungle trails and sundry other inconveniences. Solomon is soon wishing he were back in the pulpit, but it's too late now.

Years 1910-20: Elder son George develops a bad case of entrepreneurial itch. He hallucinates. Thinks his mission in life is to lay out a planned city with a world-class hotel. Dreams that someday millions will heed the clarion call to the land of Ponce de Leon. His fever is incurable.

Nov. 1924: George entices John Bowman, the "Mr. Biltmore" of hotel fame, to share in his madness.

Year 1925: Merrick and Bowman engage the New York firm of Schultze & Weaver to get cranking.

Jan. 1926: Bingo! 1500 guests assemble to celebrate the Biltmore debut—the $10-million embodiment of a pipe dream.

Sept. 1926: The worst hurricane in Florida history blows away the wind gauge—and the hotel trade.

Year 1927: The Florida land boom is also gone with the wind.

These two traumas in successive years were nearly fatal, and drove the Biltmore Corporation to bankruptcy in 1929. A financial angel came to the rescue in 1931: Col. Henry Doherty. Two months later, John Bowman was dead. Doherty's wealth was able to keep the hotel afloat for seven years. Then another rescue was needed—this time a friend and associate, George MacDonald, took the tiller and not a moment too soon, because the next year Doherty died.

During these times of peril, Merrick was subsisting with a patronage appointment as Postmaster for Miami. He died in March 1942. He ploughed $100 million (give or take a few) into his Coral Gables dream and the Biltmore. The timing of his death was merciful, no doubt, because a few months later Uncle Sam seized the Biltmore for a war hospital. The government paid Mr. MacDonald $875,000 walking money, a painful markdown from $10 million.

March 1968: U.S. closes up shop, walks away from another war casualty. Bats and bugs set up housekeeping in the emptiness.

Year 1971: The Coral Gables Preservationists to the rescue. It takes time and patience and exasperation, but they wrestle the Feds to the mat.

Year 1972: The Nixon Administration inaugurates the Historic Monument Act and is stricken with magnanimity; they make Coral Gables an offer it can't refuse—$1 and Julie Nixon Eisenhower to deliver the deed in person.

Jan. 1987: Coral Gables spruces up its one-dollar purchase with a $50 million facelift and body job . . . and throws one big welcome-back party.

Thereafter: Lucky lodgers checked in where General Eisenhower, the Duke and Duchess of Windsor, Howard Hughes, Gene Tunney, Al Capone and thousands of notables have all left big footprints.

How do I know all of this, you ask? A talented journalist who also loves this hotel, Helen Muir, has scripted the Biltmore's story in a book published by Pickering Press. In it, she relates a saga to upstage the Perils of Pauline.

George Merrick dreamed the impossible dream. Unlike the swarm of land hucksters that descended on Florida, Merrick's pitch had real substance. His plans were grand; however, his timing was off. He was thirty years too soon. He foresaw the boom but not the bust. Nor the hurricane. Successively lucky and unlucky, wealthy and unwealthy. A beautiful Florida city was his quest. He attained it posthumously.

Merrick and I were both preachers' kids. We each had fathers who pulled stakes in search of a better climate. We each wanted to become writers, but instead wound up trying to roll back the wilderness. George Merrick and his dad bought 160 acres of Florida brushland sight unseen; I bought an Alaska fish site—also unseen. But there our similarity ends. George Merrick built a magnificent hotel. I only luxuriated therein.

The Biltmore has seen parades of wedding parties, gala parties have danced in its ballrooms, and its spacious grounds and golf course have witnessed historic events. Its swimming pool is big enough to float Ari Onassis' yacht, and has been the movie set for Esther Williams and Johnny Weismuller. Filming for movies and television is routine.

Access to the Biltmore from Vizcaya and Miami Airport is easy. Its double-size rooms are quiet; it is away from traffic noise and congestion. Your "Premier" room offers a safe and robes, and the bathroom has a shaving mirror, phone, scale, hair dryer and bath towels big enough to double-wrap Willard Scott. The hotel's present management, Premier Resorts & Hotels, are real pros. I hope someday they will add Mrs. Muir's book to the room accessories. Good bedtime reading.

High above, with a panoramic view of Miami, is the Biltmore's Premier dining room. The tables are beautifully set with flowers and silver service, and the waiters are attentive.

One fine morning, amidst these surroundings, I noted an attractive young family, a foursome who resembled the Keatons of "Family Ties." I learned that they had been living in the Biltmore for eleven weeks while they awaited availability of their new home. Their impatience was showing. I know nothing about the family, but I can state that their dislocation is in enviable comfort. I also know that they are rich—I know because Suleyman the Magnificent, Sultan of the Ottoman Empire, could not have bought such lavish living with all of his wealth. Nor could any of the rich until recently; not until the advent of climate control and hot runningwater and elevators and telephones and ice. What a place to be homeless!

"Ca'd'Zan," home of John and Mabel Ringling, Sarasota, Florida

5

Circus Galleries
John Ringling

". . . you want my history. Why, I have none. I am merely John Ringling, age 39. I am one of the five brothers Ringling, sons of a Chicago merchant whose fortune was severely injured by a fire. We turned out to work, and being musical, started public concerts. In the summer we worked a circus and did well. At the present day—well, I must not talk big—we are the Ringling Brothers who employ and control a staff of 3500 people and own 400 railway cars."

-interview by "Variety", London 1908

CIRCUS DAY IN OLDEN TIMES

It is an hour before sunup in Wichita, and a little boy's father stands over the bed announcing, "The time has come!" The boy jumps up eagerly, for it is a special day. They hurry hand-in-hand along the sidewalks, joined by others, all moving excitedly toward the railroad yards.

This is CIRCUS DAY, the best day of the summer. I know—because I was the little boy.

Even before daylight, four long trains were surrounded by hundreds of workers off-loading two hundred big, bright red wagons. Lumbering elephants were everywhere, tugging at lines, following some sort of silent commands. There were cages with wild animals and clusters of horses being groomed and harnessed. One train was just Pullman cars, a rolling hotel for 1400 workers and (probably) sleepy performers. I watched with amazement as the first wagons started weaving down a dirt road toward the vacant hay field where they would set up the travelling restaurant that daily served thousands of meals to the circus troupers. I learned a lot later that some of these wagons carried 200,000 square feet of canvas that must be assembled like a jigsaw puzzle, and fast! Would they make it? Would I really be watching clowns and jugglers, trapeze flyers and elephants dancing in just a few hours? Seemed impossible—except it was Ringling Brothers, Barnum and Bailey. Those names together spelled M-A-G-I-C! And MAGIC is what this small boy saw.

John Ringling's philosophy was written when he was fifty-three years old and had thirty-five years of circus life behind him:

> " . . . The psychology of the circus really is simple: Our appeal is to the elemental instincts, to the child that is in every man. What they call 'the lure of the circus' is merely the great unexpressed yearning of every human being to be young again. The circus is a drop of water from Ponce de Leon's spring. It takes people back to childhood for two hours, and makes them boys and girls again, makes them forget as nothing else will do . . . The humorist makes fun of the man who borrows a small boy to take to the circus; to us in the business this is not funny. We see two things in it—the universal protest against growing old and the desire to give pleasure to others. A man or a woman enjoys the circus because the child enjoys it. Their great pleasure is in giving the child pleasure. The great pleasure of a circus man is that he gives pleasure to others . . . "

The five (later seven) Ringling Brothers from Baraboo, Wisconsin, were a rare team. Seldom in history has such a large family shared a single goal and worked in such harmony.

Not until the Normandy invasion would there be another logistical feat to match it. Not until Disneyland would there be another extravaganza of such magnitude—but Disney doesn't parade down Main Street a few hours after assembling a jillion-piece circus set from 200 railway flatcars. What a kit! What a thrill!

The railroad circus was unending drama with its economic ups and downs, cliff-hanger scheduling, cantankerous humans, mud, fires, money troubles, local politics, sickness and death. But come hell or high water, the show did go on—and it was the GREATEST SHOW ON EARTH!

Here at Sarasota, Florida, at the Ringling's fabulous bayfront estate where the circus made its winter quarters (after a cold start in Baraboo), I can enter the Circus Galleries and my memories spring to life.

The Ringling spread took two years to complete at a 1926 cost of $1,500,000 (1990's equivalent is $33,000,000), and that figure doesn't include the rare tapestries, works of art, musical rarities and countless treasures.

The Ringling plans were birthed at the time James Deering, the owner of Vizcaya across the peninsula, died. The Ringling house-warming took place ten years to the day after James Deering's occupancy of Vizcaya. Is there a mystical connection between these two Venetian reincarnations? Both are legacies to the people of Florida. Was fate pulling strings?

The Ringling home duplicates the facade of the Doges Palace, with the tower of the old Madison Square Garden tucked in. It is fronted with an 8000-square-foot marble terrace enclosed by terra cotta balustrades facing the bay. Standing there, I could easily imagine gondolas gliding by. Indeed, Mrs. Ringling moored hers there. It was easy to picture a covey of ships arriving from Italy bearing the accessories to recreate a Venetian Renaissance.

One might think that making a fortune through real estate transactions, railroads and the world's foremost circus would be occupation enough. Not so. John Ringling and his wife, Mable Burton Ringling, amassed more than 10,000 paintings, statues, tapestries and the like from all over the world. Much of it is now housed in a museum built in 1927 with the specific intention of bequeathing it and its art to the people of Florida.

The Ringling estate now consists of several buildings: the Art Museum, the Ca'd'Zan Residence, the Circus Galleries and a theater.

Today it is the official State Art Museum. Here there are works by Rubens, Cranach, Poussin, Hals, Van Dyke, da Cortona, Guercino, and others who worked primarily from the late sixteenth century through the mid-eighteenth—a period generally described as that of Baroque. The Asolo Theater's interior from Asolo, Italy, was re-assembled at the museum in the early 1950's and installed in its own building.

The Circus Galleries display a fascinating collection of circus memorabilia, including costumes, rare prints and drawings, calliopes and parade wagons.

As for the circus, by 1929 John, the sole surviving brother, solved a problem that had bugged the brothers throughout their circus career: how to out-fox competitors. (There were always so many of them.) Ringling bought out his competition and merged the pack. He finally became THE GRAND RINGMASTER. How sad that his brothers could not witness this coup. The merger coincided with Mrs. Ringling's death and with the start of the Great Depression. John Ringling died seven years later, in 1936.

What a brief time they had at their "winter home," and how lucky for all of us that the Ringlings left their home and art museum to Florida. To be an invited guest here—such good fortune!

If, as a child, you ever stood on the street when the circus parade passed in full revue to lure you to the BIG TOP, you can, here at Sarasota, relive that youth-time ecstasy.

Ringling is gone. His "railroad circus" is gone. But the memory lingers on at Sarasota, Florida! But the best news is at Baraboo, Wisconsin.

Circus World Museum

If the parade of olden times passed you by, a replay is do-able. It is now encapsulated by a salute to *all* circuses at Baraboo, 45 minutes north of Madison, Wisconsin. This state is the Mother of Circuses, having spawned upwards of one-hundred.

The town of Baraboo was the launching pad for the Ringling

Brothers. The Circus World Museum is located on the site of the Ringling's original winter quarters. For this legacy we have John M. Kelley, Irvin Feld, and the State Historical Society of Wisconsin to thank.

This museum is no small town gimmick. A big surprise and a bigger delight, it is the world's largest collection of circus wagons. Visitors can tour a football-field-sized pavilion that brings it all back to life.

Every July the Circus World Museum collects its antiquities and dispatches them to the iron rails. Twenty or so flatcars loaded with seventy-five restored circus wagons cross the Wisconsin landscape along a 200-mile loop past Madison, Janesville, Kenosha and up to Milwaukee, where it all culminates in a real live genuine CIRCUS PARADE! Ben Barkin, a volunteer stalwart, annually raises over $1 million in support of this event. (The appendix for this chapter tells how to verify the date.)

"Backward, turn backward, oh time in your flight . . .
make me a child again, just for tonight."

NOTE: A short distance west of the Circus Museum, near Spring Green, Wisconsin, is a "must-see" with a misleading name, *House on the Rock*. Maybe a house on a rock once upon a time, but over the years Alex Jordan went wild. Your visit will easily consume two or three hours—enough to allow your head to spin out of control.

6

Jekyll Island
(the Winter Newport)
The Cloister
(Resort)

One can get overdosed on mansions. Full-starch parties can cause an itch. Turn-of-the-century rich suffered from party-itis. The winters in Newport and Manhattan were beastly. A hide-out—please! Ah-h, relief is only a thousand miles south. A mere two days and nights by private rail car, three or four days by yacht—same guest list, same actors, now camping out.

> "To live on an island! Who among us but has felt the fascination of this idea? From the youngster playing his first game of pirates and buried treasure to the oldster who is beginning to weary somewhat of the pressure of his omnipresent fellowmen, we all know the lure of the romance which life on an island suggests . . . Yet for men of imagination and means, the improbable is not always the impossible; and the Jekyll Island Club exists today as the ingenious solution of the difficult problem of finding profound seclusion and congenial companionship in one and the same spot."
>
> Jekyll Island Club, 1916

Kids like a "club." Rich or poor, old or young, the gangs of L.A. or Harlem, or the gentry of Grosse Point or Shaker Heights—all seek a secluded haven from the demands of society and of business, from the intrusion of weirdos.

The Jekyll Island Club, formed as a hunting retreat in 1886, became the winter home for leaders of the revolution that was transforming America from an agrarian society to an industrial power.

31

The list of names included Marshall Field, James Hill, William Pulitzer, Vincent Astor, Vanderbilt, Rockefeller, and a few score other insiders who met the criteria. Actually, the club was open to nearly everyone, provided they could scrape up the $3,600 initial stock purchase, and had a siding for their private rail car or a moorage for their yacht. And it helped if a person had a few race horses or fast cars to stable.

The Jekyll Island Club opened for its first season, which might mean only two or three winter months, in January 1888. Things were a bit primitive in those days, and the rich bedded down dormitory style. Not everyone went for camping out in the dormitories with the likes of J.P. Morgan. In time, "country houses" were springing up, also the country's first condominium. Soon there were so many Manhattanites crashing the scene, one could wonder who was watching the store up north.

Then, as now, the schemers just rented a room in the Club House, except not everyone could afford $3 to $5 a day (with no meals). Even then price was an effective form of keeping the lowbrows away. As was Jekyll Creek—a sort of protective moat. World War II broke up the party. In time there would be highway access and a drawbridge for the benefit of the ICW (Inter Coastal Waterway). Modern-day commuters now stack up waiting for sail-boats to pass beneath the open bridge. We may be in a hurry, but sailboats? Never!

Nowadays, anyone wishing to emulate the rich can check in at the Jekyll Island Club, a Radisson Resort which has swallowed up $20 million or so in restoration. It's worth the cost of a night just to say you belong to the Jekyll Island Alumni.

Then shuffle back to Brunswick and over to two more islands that are modern versions of easy living: St. Simons and Sea Island.

The Sea Island Cloister

There are 32,002 reasons to choose the Cloister resort to revive your spirit. (1) It insulates you from the traffic gridlock of Orlando, (2) it isolates you from the asphalt of Las Vegas, (3) over 32,000 couples have selected it as the right place to honeymoon! If all of the spouses who have honeymooned at The Cloister would form a circle and join hands, it would set a world's record for laughter and happy memories, and perhaps explain why it was here that Eugene O'Neill wrote his only comedy.

If you honeymoon here, you can claim membership in an illustrious alumni which includes George and Barbara Bush. Also Harold and Boyce Martin. This couple returned to live permanently forty-two years later. Mr. Martin, by this time a recognized author, wrote the book—*This Happy Isle*. Read it and your visit will be richer.

Sea Island's The CLOISTER may appear to be a commercial venture because in recent times it has prospered. But its history reads more like a philanthropy. The Cloister would not have survived the depression and WWII except to preserve, at whatever expense, the dream of a Detroit industrialist.

About 1912, Howard Coffin wandered south from Michigan and discovered the Georgia Island of Sapelo. By the early twenties he was romantically involved with the nearby island of Saint Simons. Come 1926 it was a love affair with adjoining Sea Island and the world-class hotel he would build there. His industrial base in Detroit was jilted for keeps. As with lots of love affairs, his was blind, deaf and dumb. There were just a lot of no-nos. His island had no civilized access, there were lions and tigers and bears, there was a depression just around the corner.

Luckily, Mr. Coffin had a young and smart cousin, an understudy, to join him in his folly. Alfred S. (Bill) Jones, thirty years junior to his cousin, shared the vision to lead the struggling venture into the promised land.

Howard Coffin was born in 1873 into a Quaker work ethic. His engineering-prone mind was just the ticket for the emerging auto era. He most surely would have had an automobile named for him, except "COFFIN" would have been a marketing disaster. So Coffin's car was called a Chalmers, and later a Hudson. It bought a lot of Detroit real estate and made Mr. Coffin very rich. Had he stayed in the game, we must assume his saga might read like Ford's or Iacocca's. Except his love affair with the Georgia islands changed his life.

Coffin bought Sea Island in 1926 for a mere $350,000. (It sold for $500 in 1814. That's a decent appreciation.) There Coffin would build his dream hotel, and that's where his money would disappear. At Sea Island his friends would congregate and be renewed. Movers and shakers of the industrial revolution would meet, along with artists and writers and singers and world leaders, and it would be beautiful! Except Coffin's nest egg ran out.

Addison Mizner, already famous for his Florida feats, and already in land-bust trouble, was the ideal designer. Mizner would even be able to bring along the name from his Boca Raton triumph (money-eating alligator)—The Cloister was underway on Sea Island.

Big people have big dreams. This dream was far too big. Except Bill Jones was on deck. And although Coffin's strength ran out (soon after his money), his young cousin was in the fight to the finish.

By 1928 there was an impressive start. Bill Jones was now president of the venture and married to a Dayton lady, Kit Talbot. President Calvin Coolidge planted a live oak and led a parade of newsworthy guests. The oak has since grown to be a giant—as has the reputation of The Cloister. Together they weathered many a storm.

The first decade was a time of relentless anxiety. The great depression was a nightmare; Howard Coffin's wife died in 1932, a remarriage went sour for Coffin, his stock tumbled, debts defaulted, properties were lost. He died childless in 1937, took his own life, and can never know that his dark clouds now have a silver lining for those of us fortunate enough to discover The Cloister.

Despite the travail of its adolescent years, The Cloister is now in the winners circle. Bill Jones, and his son who has now succeeded him, have created a Mobil five-star resort. AAA rates it five diamonds. It offers golf courses (fifty-four holes) about which Bobby Jones has boasted, there are eighteen superb clay tennis courts, a beach club for lunching and sunning, a river for fishing and lazing, bridle trails, meeting rooms for tea and cards, evening dancing. Or you can do nothing. Not really nothing, because at The Cloister you've turned the clock back to an era when gracious living was an activity.

This is the place to form memories. Therefore, the next visit by my wife and me will be as honeymooners. Where is it written in concrete that a honeymoon can't be repeated, even after fifty years? And if we're lucky enough to be a "1,000th," the week will be free. Maybe we'll honeymoon here frequently and improve those odds.

In 1928, Howard Coffin looked around him and said:

> *"Here is a country lovely and unspoiled. Here is a simple and satisfying restfulness . . . a place to charm the mind while nature mends nerves worn thin by living too fast and too hard. Here in short is peace and play and freedom."*

If such was a truism in 1928, in this last decade of the 20th century it deserves to be bronzed.

POSTSCRIPT: Reservations at The Cloister tend to be tight. If the visitor's timing is wrong, there is a great option: The King and Prince Beach Resort on St. Simons Island. This illustrious Hotel has a storied history and a regal atmosphere to support its name. The King and Prince has all the facilities a vacationer could hope for, including indoor and outdoor pools, and of course the Atlantic Ocean with miles of sandy beach. See the Appendix for toll-free numbers for all three lodgings in this chapter.

The Vanderbilt Family

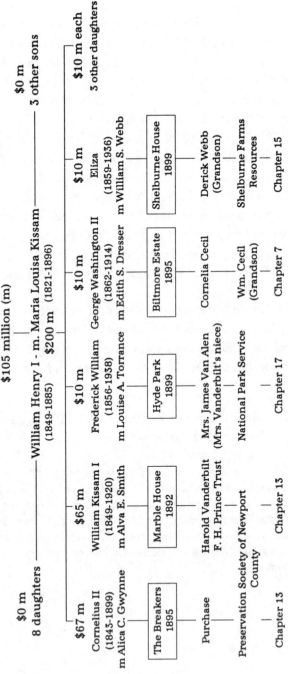

Cornelius Vanderbilt ("The Commodore") - married (m.) Sophia Johnson
(1794-1877)   (1797-1868)

$105 million (m)

William Henry I - m. Maria Louisa Kissam
(1849-1885)   (1821-1896)
$200 m

$0 m
8 daughters

$0 m
3 other sons

$10 m each
3 other daughters

$67 m	$65 m	$10 m	$10 m	$10 m
Cornelius II (1843-1899) m Alica C. Gwynne	William Kissam I (1849-1920) m Alva E. Smith	Frederick William (1856-1938) m Louise A. Torrance	George Washington II (1862-1914) m Edith S. Dresser	Eliza (1859-1936) m William S. Webb
The Breakers 1895	Marble House 1892	Hyde Park 1899	Biltmore Estate 1895	Shelburne House 1899
Purchase	Harold Vanderbilt F. H. Prince Trust	Mrs. James Van Alen (Mrs. Vanderbilt's niece)	Cornelia Cecil	Derick Webb (Grandson)
Preservation Society of Newport County		National Park Service	Wm. Cecil (Grandson)	Shelburne Farms Resources
Chapter 13	Chapter 13	Chapter 17	Chapter 7	Chapter 15

The "William Henry" Branch
—the "third-generation" mansions in this book—

Biltmore (Estate)

Think "Vanderbilt"—think "MANSION!" The third-generation Vanderbilts own that word. The five estates diagrammed with this chapter are survivors of a breathtaking era of opulence. Architectural extravagance that dazzled the Eastern seaboard. Scattered remnants still spice up the landscape, but most have succumbed to the wrecking ball. The family tree pictured may help portray the branch through which most of the wealth flowed and how its status symbols have been gifted to the public domain.

Nothing in the behavior of generations I and II prepared the country for the spending spree of the grandkids.

The family epic started like any other story of immigrant-family-makes-good. There was this hardworking Dutch family on Staten Island with lots of kids. One of whom, Cornelius, was a go-getter. A tough lad with no time for school. By age sixteen he'd wormed his way into the business world with a small boat, raking in fares to cross New York Bay. He worked hard, expanded, roughed up the competition, expanded, worked, expanded. It's actually a simple story, and presumably if an "eager beaver" keeps it up long enough and is in the right spot at the right time in history, he can accumulate $100 million. Anyway, Cornelius did.

In time, Cornelius, nicknamed "The Commodore," had thirteen children and even more railroads. Of the children, only one son, William Henry, worked into his father's respect. Girls didn't count, and in fact didn't even qualify for the family mausoleum if their name changed from Vanderbilt by marriage. The old Commodore was not a sentimentalist.

Favored son William H. married Maria Louisa Kissam, daughter of a Dutch Reform clergyman. William gradually assumed control

Photo courtesy of Biltmore Estate, Asheville North Carolina

of the railroads, including the New York Central, built Grand Central Station and became a power in Manhattan. In 1877 he came into possession of most of his father's wealth—$100 million. When W.H. died, he left over $200 million to his eight offspring.

This third generation is notorious. Described in the family tree shown here, they showed the world how to dispose of money as effectively as their father and grandfather showed how to make it.

Vanderbilt wealth converts to billions in 1990s money. Had there been a Forbes 400 then, they'd have ranked #1. They would have made Donald Trump look cautious, Harold Simmons look timid, Ted Turner slow (on both land and water).

For a few decades around the turn of the century, Vanderbilts grabbed the headlines. Only one third-generation Vanderbilt wanted to get away from it all. The youngest son of William Henry yearned for the quiet life. George Washington Vanderbilt II didn't fit into the Newport-Manhattan social whirl. He preferred to browse in book stores, settle down with great authors, get serious.

George W., among Vanderbilts, was the scholar. He traveled extensively, spoke eight languages fluently, and was knowledgeable in architecture and art. He knew the European sources of rare collectors items he would want for his dream home—someday.

He wished to get away from New York winters, and the Great Smoky Mountains caught his fancy. The weather was nice, people were friendly and elbow space abundant. Land in the southwest corner of North Carolina was cheap.

George had a small inheritance from his grandfather, "the Commodore," plus some birthday presents along the way. It all added up to a few million dollars—enough for a modest beginning.

George wasn't married but must have known it would happen someday. Vanderbilts didn't have much trouble finding wives, and with a house in place he'd be ready.

He started with 5,000 acres of wooded hill and dale to insure privacy, but soon ran his holdings up to two-hundred square miles. That's enough to make a national forest, and in time it did.

Anyone who ever built a house knows that things snowball. The end result is always more than the beginning plan, and always over budget. This happened with George. Just a kid in a candy store. He had a great architect and landscape designer, and together they had great ideas. Soon they were running about Europe checking out the creations of royalty. Excitement mounted and, who knows how, things got out of hand.

The Biltmore grew to harmonize with the size of the property—and the height of Mount Pisgah off in the distance. It took most of the nearby town of Asheville to keep construction moving. Trainloads of stone moved in on the Vanderbilt siding. Thousands of workmen were needed. For Asheville it was a basic industry for five years, and ongoing.

It deserved a name. George chose "Bildt" for the town of his Dutch forebears, and "more," which is olde English for "rolling up-land country." Lacking this briefing, a visitor might assume the name derived from "build-more" (and more . . . and more . . .).

Near the end of 1895, George's dream cottage was ready for partial occupancy . . . and why not a house-warming party? Christmas. It was a long way for the tribe to travel—even in private railroad cars that chugged right up to the Biltmore gate. Their eyeballs must have popped. George, the family kid who ran away from the mansion crowd, had out-mansioned them all!

The dream cottage was now ready to bedazzle a damsel. George did marry (as you suspected he might) in 1898. He chose Edith Stuyvesant Dresser, a descendant of *the* Peter Stuyvesant. Nice choice for both; kept it Dutch. In August of 1900, their first and only child, Cornelia, was born.

The dream cottage, now a reality, was a true extravaganza! Who's to blame? Or who gets the credit? The answer hangs upstairs on the walls of the Living Hall: portraits of Richard Morris Hunt and Frederick L. Olmstead. Key building and grounds designers in other Vanderbilt creations, and friends with George from youth (George wanted the best and he picked a prime team), he liked and trusted them. So much so that he brought John Singer Sargent to the Biltmore to do their portraits. These two men rank at the top in their professions. There's a sad, sad footnote: Hunt died right after the sitting (actually he's standing). The artist's portrayal gives an inkling of his condition. His death was a few weeks short of the 1895 Christmas christening. He was cheated by death from seeing the culmination of five years' work. His son finished the job.

This sketchy book cannot do justice to the 250 rooms and a thousand acres of landscaping. A map is inadequate and the following is merely a sampling:

The Tapestry Gallery: It is ninety feet long and lined with collector items, among them three Brussels tapestries woven early in the 16th century. They depict Gothic symbolism with figures taken from Greek and Roman mythology, and from the Bible and Apocrypha. There are three large portraits: two by Sargent and one by Giovanni Boldini.

Let's move to George's favorite room—The Library. It contains over 20,000 beautifully-bound books that reflect George Vanderbilt's interests. We are assured that Mr. V. read voraciously. The black marble fireplace is mounted with carvings. In fact, there are carvings in every direction. When I first saw it, the ceiling made me gasp. It is a full-area mural, "*The Chariot of Aurora*," brought to America from the Pisani Palace in Venice. A wood-carved circular staircase ascends to an upper walkway that accesses more books! And still more books! As with George, I decided this would be MY favorite room—until I moved to the next room.

The Banquet Hall: Already gorged on opulence, the visitor comes upon a banquet table set for thirty under a seventy-foot ceiling. A score of flags, including those of the thirteen colonies, fly high overhead. The size of this room would swallow the first four houses my wife and I owned. (In Alaska we built small to conserve on muscle and fuel.) There's a massive fireplace at the end of the room I could park my car in. It is said the acoustics are perfect. Good. A guest needn't shout to have the gravy passed.

Upstairs are thirty-one bedrooms. Below, there's a bowling alley installed by Brunswick in 1895. It may be the oldest in existence. And then there's the Hallowe'en Room. In 1926, we're told, a party was planned, and each guest came in beforehand to decorate a section of the room. It took them three weeks!

The indoor swimming pool has seventeen dressing rooms. Back then it was mainly for the ladies; the men were shooting pool. I could go on and on. I haven't even mentioned the gardens, the stable, the barn, the winery, the . . . It's something you just have to see to believe. Incidentally, though the mansion wasn't finished when George and Edith and little Cornelia moved in, it didn't crimp their life style. They had other places to go in a pinch: a mansion in Washington, D.C., a summer cottage in Bar Harbor, Maine, and, of course, a Fifth Avenue town house in New York. All Vanderbilts had one of those.

Gradually the money ran down. The estate budget was trimmed. Morris and Olmstead had each left a son to carry on as landscaper and architect. It came as something of a shock to them that the well was running dry.

In 1914, George W. Vanderbilt II died of complications following an appendectomy at the age of fifty-two, after just sixteen years of marriage. With less than a million dollars remaining, Mrs. V. deeded off land until only 12,500 acres remained. Biltmore passed to Cornelia, who had married John Francis Amherst Cecil, and then to their sons, William and George Cecil. It is William Cecil, the current owner, who invites us to visit this magnificent property and make it a cherished memory.

There is an admission charge. It is the highest for any attraction in this book, and well it should be. This is still privately owned, and expenses must be horrendous. This showplace cost Vanderbilt a mind-boggling sum in 1890! It could not be duplicated today. Where are such craftsmen?

On the grounds is the Deerpark Restaurant converted from the original dairy barn. How often do you have a chance to eat in a Richard Morris Hunt creation? There's the Stable Cafe (you can guess its origin). The "farm" supplies a store selling wines from the estate vineyards, and there are two gift shops. Eat in one of the restaurants, of course, but not too much, because I want to coax you across the valley to a memorable resort for the night where dining, of itself, will be an event while you reflect upon the lifestyle at the start of this century.

The finest Resort Hotel in the world has been built at Sunset Mountain, Asheville, N. C.

Open all the year
Absolutely Fireproof

Mr. E. W. Grove, of St. Louis, Mo., has built at Asheville, N. C., the finest resort hotel in the world Grove Park Inn. Built by hand of the great boulders of Sunset Mountain, it is full of rest and comfort and wholesomeness. The front lawn is the hundred-acre eighteen-hole golf links of the Asheville Country Club, and with it sixty acres belonging to the hotel.

The purest water obtainable is piped seventeen miles from the slopes of Mount Mitchell, over 6,000 feet altitude.

Biltmore milk and cream exclusively, supplied from 200 registered Jerseys on the estate of Mr. Geo. W. Vanderbilt. It is doubtful if this famous dairy is equaled in the world.

Five hundred feet of porche at Grove Park Inn

Four hundred one-piece rugs were made at Aubusson, France. Seven hundred pieces of furniture and over 600 lighting fixtures of solid copper made by hand by the Roycrofters.

The plumbing material is the finest that has ever been placed in any hotel in the world. Bath-tubs and fixtures all solid porcelain. No pipes visible anywhere. No radiators to be seen—all placed in recesses under windows. No electric bulbs visible.

The "Big Room," or what some call the lobby, is 80 by 120 feet, and is probably the most unique public room in the country. Two great fireplaces in it will burn twelve-foot logs.

For the golfers there are lockers and shower-bath rooms with a forty-foot swimming pool not excelled by the finest clubs in existence, and the players are less than 100 yards distant on the links.

Situated amid the most inspiring mountain scenery. Grove Park Inn offers the finest combination of climate, comfort, and happiness that we believe has ever been made possible.

Especially available for northern guests in the Spring, Fall, and Winter, going and returning from farther southern resorts, or for an all Winter resort. Persons with any form of tubercular trouble will not be received at the Inn.

Rates—American Plan $5.00 a day upward. Reached by the Southern Railway.

GROVE PARK INN

Sunset Mountain **Asheville, N. C.**

New York Booking Office, 1180 Broadway

Grove Park Inn Ad courtesy of National Geographic (1913)

8

Grove Park Inn
Asheville

You've had your day amidst the grandeur of the Biltmore Estate. Your guide has hosted you as an honored guest—vicariously, of course. Now, how do you descend from this mountaintop to the real world? With nighttime approaching, must Cinderella return to four drab walls? Not at all.

Just across the valley is a hotel that can prolong your fantasy. The Grove Park Inn is not your typical plastic roomery with a coffee maker and styrofoam. Just as George Washington Vanderbilt gave new meaning to opulence, Edwin Wiley Grove matched the pace with an edifice that came to be known as "the finest resort hotel in the world." Granted, that accolade is claimed by grand hotels all over creation, but I believe that nothing less than the Grove Park Inn is suitable for easing out of your Biltmore trance.

Mr. Grove was the owner of a pharmaceutical firm in St. Louis that produced the famous label, "Grove's Bromo Quinine." He was drawn to Asheville—perhaps the same attraction that snared George Vanderbilt—and there he chose a location on Sunset Mountain, opposite "the Estate," to build his unique resort.

The architect? There was none. Mr. Grove, it appears, was unable to convey his dream to those he consulted, so he turned to his son-in-law, Fred L. Seely, who supervised construction, and ultimately ran the business under a lease. What an in-law! What a creation! A rock-hound heaven! The stone work is so prolific it boulders you over. Italian masons heaped it together. Construction began in 1912, and in less than a year—behold! A world class hotel.

Word of mouth soon attracted a procession of notable and wealthy persons. William Jennings Bryan, the silver-tongued orator, delivered an opening address, and the guest book would, in time, register Thomas Edison, Henry Ford, John D. Rockefeller, Jr.;

Presidents Wilson, Taft, Coolidge, Hoover, Roosevelt and Eisenhower. Guests included composer Bela Bartok, writers such as Scott Fitzgerald, soloist Enrico Caruso, Mount Rushmore sculptor, Gutzon Borglum, and the Mayo brothers.

It was a different era. Legend tells of Irvin Cobb being admonished to lower his voice in the lobby. Hotel literature set the tone: "We do not entertain children. Not that we dislike children, but we wish to maintain a place where tired, busy people may get away from excitement and all annoyances and rest their nerves." Pamper their bodies, too, as evidenced by "apple-a-day" baskets of wrapped fruit, passed through the lobby after each mealtime.

A custom at that time was to present all change at the cashier's window in crisp new paper money and washed and polished silver. Amazing?

Who could resist this 1913 invitation to the finest resort hotel in the world? There've been many changes since 1913. In 1955, Mr. and Mrs. Charles Sammons of Dallas acquired the property and began a major remodeling and enlargement which added convention facilities and the adjoining Country Club of Asheville.

Go to Grove Park Inn with the Biltmore Estate still fresh in your memory. Browse along its foyers, loiter in its massive lobby, dine on its Sunset Terrace and ponder the footprints left here since 1913. Remember those with whom you are sharing this unusual place. You'll think bigger and leave stronger.

Photo courtesy of Grove Park Inn, Asheville, North Carolina

Photo courtesy of The Homestead, Hot Springs, Virginia

9

Monticello / Virginia
From Homestead to Williamsburg

History intertwines with most of the attractions in this book—and none more so than Monticello, the home Thomas Jefferson built in Virginia. No state has furnished more Presidents to the USA and of such stature. There is no soil in our country more sacred than Virginia's. I doubted my ability to pay Jefferson proper tribute, and asked my true blue-gray Virginian niece for help. Her response: " . . . I do sort of worship the man, although Lord knows why, because along with great qualities he was dreadfully arrogant, often single focused and judgmental, not particularly sensitive to women, and he couldn't handle money very effectively . . . ."
She wrote as follows:

Monticello and Thomas Jefferson

Monticello provides a setting that expresses the depth and the breadth of a remarkable American—Thomas Jefferson. His contributions far exceed those limited accomplishments depicted in history books, and his legacy is tied to a remarkable period in both American, and, more specifically, Virginian history.

Each state or region has its own peculiar character, and Virginia's is exemplified by its umbilical ties to a noble heritage. Virginians speak with pride about what was, and the state is a veritable monument to the events and people that created our greatest political triumph—the American revolution—and our most abysmal failure—the Civil War. Virginians are quick to remind you that their ancestors presided at the birth of this nation and provided some of our most outstanding leaders, including five presidents.

Thomas Jefferson is considered the quintessential

Virginian. As a member of the gentry, an author, botanist, wine maker, inventor, lawyer, farmer, governor, ambassador and president, he exemplified the scope of what man could achieve.

Visitors to Monticello, Jefferson's home for over fifty years, may be surprised not only by what it is, but also by what it is not. It's a southern plantation but without the familiar white, rectangular manor house immortalized by books and movies. It's the home of an educated aristocrat. Yet the attraction of Monticello is not its opulence but its architectural precision, the practicality of design and the genuine livableness of the home. While some historic homes emphasize grandeur and style, at Monticello one is treated to simplicity and innovation. The entrance hall houses a huge (working) seven-day calendar clock thought to be designed by Jefferson. It uses a system of cannon-ball weights and defies conventional interior decor rules, because it required cutting a hole in the floor to accommodate its size. In his library sits a duplicating writing device that allowed him to make personal copies of all his writing. He had questions and strong opinions on every conceivable subject, and his writing exceeded 40,000 pieces. Each room of the home and the surrounding out-buildings and grounds offer insight into a private life and define a man of invention who was constantly re-examining his world and devising solutions for myriad questions. His remarkable energy and his creative ability to communicate his thoughts with passion and clarity enabled him to become a popular public figure.

Jefferson was born into money and position. His father's death, however, severely restrained the family income and Jefferson, although generally comfortable and at times a generous spender, was never a wealthy man and was often in debt. He attended William & Mary College in Williamsburg, studying law under the renowned George Wythe, and was admitted to the Virginia bar in 1767. Three years later he moved to his unfinished mountaintop retreat nestled in the verdant Virginia hills over-looking Charlottesville. Monticello, the Indian word for "little mountain," would ultimately become the perfect monument to this unique man of ideas, letters and vision. He designed the home and the grounds, and supervised work on his creation throughout his lifetime. Specific work began on the grounds in 1767, when Jefferson was twenty-five. The mountain top was leveled in 1768, and construction on the house began in 1770. He lived there a short time as a bachelor, and then brought his new bride, Martha Wagles Skelton, to Monticello in 1772.

Jefferson was a voracious reader with an inquiring, scientific mind. He spent a great deal of his time at Monticello reading about, and experimenting with, types of plants and hybrids. During his life, he was continually pulled between his love of the quiet, productive life at Monticello and his sense of duty and call to give philosophical leadership to an emerging nation that needed his mind and energy.

In 1775, he reluctantly left Monticello for Philadelphia to serve as a member of the first Continental Congress. It was here that he contributed the first of what Jefferson considered his three most significant achievements—the Declaration of Independence. Fresh from his work with the Continental Congress, Jefferson came home to accept a term in the Virginia House of Delegates. His mind was rich with the eloquent ideas needed to nourish a budding nation. It was as a delegate that Jefferson wrote what he considered his second document worthy of remembrance—the Virginia Statute of Religious Freedom. This Statute was the first legislative mandate recognizing that religious thoughts and actions were of a totally personal nature, beyond the legitimate scope and concern of the government. With this document, Jefferson created a specific separation between church and state. His ideals became Virginia law in 1786, and were incorporated into the First Amendment of the Bill of Rights of the United States Constitution in 1790.

It is especially fitting that legal precedent for religious tolerance was created in the Commonwealth of Virginia, the State that is now home to the Edgar Cayce Association for Research and Enlightenment, Pat Robertson's Christian Broadcast Network, the Old Time Gospel of Jerry Falwell . . . and Swannanoa atop the Blue Ridge mountains of Virginia.

While a member of the House of Delegates, Jefferson accepted the role of Governor, a position he held (to no great distinction) during much of the Revolutionary War. It was to the frustration of many of his colleagues that he chose to spend a good deal of his time at his beloved Monticello. His wife, Martha, was in failing health and died tragically in 1782. Mr. Jefferson never remarried, although he appears to have enjoyed the company of women.

Instead, he tightened his connection with his daughter, Martha, who later served as his official hostess and companion.

There is considerable evidence that his time in France fed his interest in architecture, design, culture, fine living and wine. His experiences in France were translated throughout Monticello. He had early planted an extensive grape arbor and, upon his return, he further experimented with grapes and wine.

It is as the third president of the U.S., following the term of John Adams, that most Americans know Thomas Jefferson. His insight and quest for knowledge enabled the purchase and exploration of a vast part of the American west (now memorialized at St. Louis and written about in Chapter twenty-two).

For most of Jefferson's life, Monticello was in a constant state of "remodeling." Throughout his tenure as Secretary of State and Vice President, and finally as President, Jefferson supervised creative additions. An all-weather passageway was completed, a north pavilion added, and the dome that beckons to visitors as the centerpiece for the house was constructed.

He spent his final years seeking the peace that Monticello offered, and continuing his lifetime quest of knowledge and meaning. At one time there were about 6,000 books on his shelves, spanning his interest in horticulture, astronomy and philsophy. They were sold to the federal government in 1815 to become the nucleus of the new Library of Congress.

His final great pursuit was the creation of the University of Virginia. He designed the buildings, including the now famous rotunda and "the Lawn" that stretches out from it, and helped develop a rigorous curriculum and faculty. The University opened its doors to students in 1825. It was this third accomplishment for which Mr. Jefferson wished to be remembered.

Thomas Jefferson died at Monticello on July 4, 1826, the 50th anniversary of the signing of the Declaration of Independence. It is a final date he shares with colleague and friend, John Adams. Adams also died on that day with his final words reputed to be, "Jefferson still lives." A statement no one familiar with his life and words can refute!

- Jo Bedard

A missing link in the Monticello story was supplied by my mentor in Jeffersonian history, Professor Borden. How did this national shrine become accessible to the public?

It was not willed by Jefferson, nor preserved by our government. It was saved by a maverick naval officer, Lieutenant Uriah Levy. He purchased it from James Barclay, who had bought it as distress property from Jefferson's daughter, Martha Jefferson Randolph. In November 1831, when debts had overwhelmed her, she lowered her price from $71,000 to $7,000. Barclay's interest was not in history, but in producing silkworms with mulberry trees. When his scheme fizzled, Lt. Levy rescued the property.

With a reverence for Jefferson, Uriah Levy had the dedication and money to restore Monticello. However, being a northerner and a Jew did not endear him to the local gentry. He spent most of his time in New York, where his real estate was doing nicely and his naval commission and ethnic background were not impediments.

Uriah, by now Commodore Levy, wanted Monticello to belong to the people. "I give, devise and bequeath my Farm and Estate at Monticello in Virginia . . . to the people of the United States . . . " That was his wish when he signed his will in 1858. Congress, slow in acting, allowed the clock to run out. Levy's heirs had time to contest and break the will.

Monticello slid into the doldrums until 1879, when a nephew of Uriah's, Jefferson Levy, bought it from the heirs at $10,500. It was once again in the hands of a friend who invested heavily in restoration.

Over the years, there were frequent agitations to salvage Monticello. Congress twiddled its thumbs. Finally a citizen group formed the Thomas Jefferson Memorial Foundation, and purchased the estate from J.M. Levy for $500,000. This was nearly 100 years after Jefferson's death.

Monticello was finally secure, and Jefferson's grave was safe from public whimsy and vandalism.

If your visit to this national shrine is a treasured experience, give thanks to the memory of Uriah and Jefferson Levy, and to the citizenry who nurtured the Thomas Jefferson Memorial Foundation. By the way, you can give more than thanks. Their needs are on-going, and they will welcome a tax-deductible contribution . . . thereafter you can feel like one of the faithful. (See Appendix—Chapter 9)

Having soaked in the fascination of a President's unique creation, we also have opportunity to soak in the same mineral springs as have half the Presidents from Washington's time forward. A scenic drive, two hours or so toward the setting sun, and we can cavort at a resort—two of them in fact—that have been gathering places for the power structure dating from Revolutionary War times.

The GREENBRIER and The HOMESTEAD are both five-star rated and share many distinctions. Both are so deep into the outback it takes an Indian tracker to serve a subpoena. Both have mineral springs/baths/spas. Both have thousands of acres for elbow room, riding and hiking; PGA golf courses and lots of tennis courts. Both have dress codes well-deserved by their elegance, and both are in the National Register of Historical places.

These are *destination resorts*, not overnight highway stops. They are expensive, with facilities and services and staff to merit a dent in your travel budget. If you're only going around once, take your finery and go for it.

The Homestead at Hot Springs, Virginia

Schedule to arrive here before four, and unwind over complimentary high tea. Register between mid-December and March, and you may ski. Even at night! Surprised? Virginia isn't on the winter-resort circuit, but modern innovation has brought snow guns, so in the Appalachian Mountains at a low base elevation of 2500 feet, there are lifts . . . and enough vertical drop (700 feet) to permit a twisted ankle or broken leg and all those fun things.There is ice skating, too!

George Washington came here in 1761 to "soak in the waters." The first Homestead was built ten years later. It had no plumbing other than a few public toilets, heat was by open fires and lighting from oil lamps. Jefferson came also, and we can be sure he contributed to the design. The modern era began when the Ingalls family purchased the property, and in 1901 opened the now famous Kentucky brick hotel. It has been enlarged and improved to keep pace with the times.

Homestead guests are received in The Great Hall, where they move between stately Corinthian columns. It is a magnificent room with charming old-world decor, aided by two fireplaces that exude warmth and hospitality. This is where your tea will be served to the accompaniment of a musical concert. Your service will be fairly close to the style which attracted most of the notables described in this book, including nine U.S. presidents, from Taft to Johnson. Lord and Lady Astor honeymooned here, as did Woodrow Wilson for his second romance. Sam Snead is the golf pro.

The Ingalls family has owned this property for a century, and that means they've hosted a lot of history-makers. Melville E. Ingalls is the presiding family member at this writing.

Don't spend all of your euphoria here, because a few miles further, across the state line into West Virginia, is a resort to call up adjectives I don't possess. You, too, may run out of words to describe . . .

Photo Courtesy of The Greenbriar, White Sulphur Springs, West Virginia

The Greenbrier at White Sulphur Springs

Behold, a legendary American resort combining two centuries of history with classic architecture, inspired interiors, unlimited activities and impeccable service. You name it and it's here: championship par-72 golf courses (Ryder Cup and Senior PGA Tour), and tennis facilities to rank among the country's fifty greatest.

The white sulphur springs were discovered about the time of the Revolutionary War. Early in the 1880s the famous spring house was built. It has become the resort's symbol. An architectural pattern known as Old White Cottages started in 1832, and a procession of aristocratic southern families made a ritual of drinking the waters. "Old White" became the center of conviviality wherein bourbon was discovered to be even more effective than "the waters." By 1868 Collis Huntington pushed his Chesapeake & Ohio Railroad through White Sulphur Springs, and now private rail cars could add a layer of social standing to Old White. In 1910 the C&O purchased the famous resort and started a building program that has never stopped.

The Greenbrier's eminence was gilded when Robert R. Young, Chairman of the C&O Railroad, made it his pet. He commissioned Dorothy Draper, a noted interior decorator, to set the tone and style. It became her lifetime quest.

The Greenbrier history makes it a bit oldish, yet it is so youngish it recently added a new spa and mineral bath, costing a cool $7 million.

Its ambiance has appealed to famous personages as diverse as Thomas Edison and Judy Garland. Twenty-two U.S. presidents have vacationed and attended meetings here, our bigget corporations hold strategy sessions here, and it has long been the tribal rite for eastern socialites—so that's credential enough for me.

Among the great hotel resorts of the USA, only this one can claim veteran status as a military hospital in the Civil War—on both sides! It was used by the Confederacy first, then later, as western

Virginia broke away from its parent in 1863 and rejoined the Union, by the Union forces.

The Greenbrier and the Homestead were both World War II participants in a fashion that will rock your senses. War may be hell, but there are ways to improve on it. Be a diplomat. At the outbreak of the war, while our citizenry were boiling with anger at Japanese and Germans, their diplomatic corps were bundled up by the FBI and cozily jailed in these two luxury encampments. For half a year, a thousand or so enemy diplomats and their families suffered the luxury of our nation's two top resorts, guests of the State Department for a daily tab of ten dollars per VIP. "What did you do in the war, Daddy?" Just golf and tennis and hot baths and haute cuisine—war can be such a nuisance.

The "spring house" is still there. Above it there poses a fleet-footed goddess. Some say it's Hygeia, the goddess of health. Others claim it's Hebe, the symbol of youth. Both belong at the Greenbrier . . . and so does any patriot who feels entitled to the same amenities accorded our wartime adversaries. May we drink to that?

Footnote: Colonial Williamsburg is situated between Monticello and the Brandywine Valley—hence its mention in the chapter heading. See Chapter 12 for Colonial Williamsurg—among the Rockefeller legacies.

Pennsylvania

Brandywine River

Longwood Gardens

Winterthur Museum and Gardens

Brandywine River Museum

Nemours Mansion and Gardens

Hagley Museum

Delaware Museum of Natural History

Brandywine Valley

60

10

Longwood Gardens / Nemours / Winterthur

The du Pont Duchy of Delaware

The Brandywine Valley is just another wooded, hilly, pristine bit of Eastern countryside. It's the watershed for a small and unimposing river which merges into the Christina River. As rivers go, the Brandywine would never make a sentence in Geography 101. Back about 1801, however, a young Frenchman combed the countryside for a waterpower source for an entrepreneurial dream. He happened upon the Brandywine which, in all its innocence, dropped some one hundred feet in a distance of only four miles. That'll turn a pretty good waterwheel. And so Éleuthère Irénée du Pont, youngest son of Pierre Samuel du Pont, harnessed the small river for cheap waterpower to turn the wheels to mix charcoal, sulphur and saltpeter together. With this readily salable product, he began an epic that eventually blanketed this corner of Delaware and southeastern Pennsylvania with prosperity and fame.

This second son of Pierre was endowed with a noble name meaning "liberty" and "peace." At the age of thirteen his father commanded Éleuthère Irénée to fight for the public good and to be aware that "no privilege exists which is not inseparably bound to a duty." This investiture ceremony was to be the marching order for succeeding generations: "Promise one another that you will always stand together, united, that you will comfort one another in every sorrow and distress, that you will help one another in all your endeavors, that you will stand by one another no matter what the difficulty or danger. I bless you, my children, and may heaven also bless you. Bless your labors and your children. May your families be carried on by wives who are good, sensible, courageous, economical, generous, simple and modest like the mother you have lost. May each generation of your descendants struggle unceasingly to pass on to its children a better heritage than it received."

The ceremony took place shortly after the death of the mother who had given Pierre Samuel his two sons. E.I. certainly took the oath seriously, and the ensuing generations carved the most fantastic family business dynasty ever to stand on this continent.

Today there are thousands of du Ponts—many of them cousins by the dozens who have intermarried. The du Pont dynasty ranks among the world's richest, though the family has had its share of walking on the brink.

From today's perspective, it seems laughable to think there was a time a du Pont couldn't cash a check. In the early days, father and sons suffered bankruptcy, and ethnic and religious barriers. Perseverance paid off, however, and after discarding numerous economic forays, they discovered gunpowder was to be their financial savior. Undercapitalized ($36,000) and plagued by fires and explosions—as well as deaths and injuries among the workers—the hazardous business succeeded. The family was its own fortress, and with little more than a communal handshake the du Ponts held together for one hundred years and became the economic force in Delaware.

By the turn of the 20th century, the size and success of the empire called for more structure. With a leveraged buyout modern day raiders would be proud to duplicate, the first corporate structure was created. Three fourth-generation cousins bought the venture from the family holding for a paltry $15 million. No cash down. With four percent notes and shares of stock, Alfred, Coleman and Pierre had themselves a money machine. The E.I. du Pont de Nemours and Company, with Coleman first in command and Pierre second, was headed down a fast track. The three cousins, in their thirties, held controlling ownership of the most spectacular business success in our history. Within fifteen years, it rose to billionaire status and was about to undergo massive expansion to supply explosives for WWI. The cousins (now numbering twenty or so key players) disagreed and fractured in the first interfamily litigation. The power struggle made headlines and inflicted wounds which healed slowly. Though Papa Pierre's "investiture" had held things together like a magic wand for over a century, its statute of limitations ran out.

As the years rolled on, du Pont explosives fought wars; du Pont blasting powder cleared the channel for the Panama Canal and tunnels for New York City subways, and figured in the taming of rivers and the winning of the west. Close to home, du Pont dynamite was used (or misused) by this writer to blast massive stumps out of his cutover timber land—at great peril to himself and the neighborhood.

Money buys comfort and wields power in politics and commerce, but it doesn't insulate its owners from sorrow or give immunity to heartbreak. The du Ponts have had their share of divorce, suicide and painful publicity. The family has always made great copy—as when Ethel du Pont, the granddaughter of the Company founder, married F.D. Roosevelt, Jr., son of the President of the U.S., in 1937! The marriage may not have been made in heaven, because it did fall apart after producing two children. One can imagine the schoolyard banter:

"My Mom's grandfather is richer than anybody"

"Well, my Pop's father has been elected President more often than any other—so gotcha!"

What a family!

The company doubled, then quadrupled, in size with Pierre at the helm, expanding into chemicals, synthetic fibers, cellophane and so forth. An artesian stream of welcome products poured out to an eager public. Rayon gave the ladies a fashion lift, cellophane improved food storage, freon simplified refrigeration, neoprene lessened maintenance of automobiles. And nylon! Well, that's a story by itself.

And where is the public legacy? There were (and are) mountains of money to stash away, and some of it has produced some spectacular attractions in the Brandywine Valley for the public to enjoy.

Longwood Gardens: Pierre Samuel du Pont (1870-1954), who died childless, established Longwood Gardens and endowed it with $33 million. Nestled in this valley thirty miles southwest of Philadelphia near Kennett Square, Pennsylvania, is a horticultural cornucopia created by Pierre through the twenties. The garden is so extensive and complete it requires two hundred employees plus dozens of volunteers to tend the 350 acres of plant life,fountains, conservatories and ballroom. That's right, ballroom! An exquisite setting for banquets, lectures and concerts. Elsewhere in this travel guide are great formal gardens, but none with a 10,000-pipe organ! If you're into trees and flowers and shrubs and illuminated fountain shows, Longwood is your Alpha and Omega.

Winterthur: Winterthur takes its name from an old Swiss city, the ancestral home of an early du Pont investor whose son married a daughter of Éleuthère Irénée, bought the land from the du Pont family, then sold it back to the family in 1865. In 1880, Henry Francis du Pont was born in the dwelling which evolved into the Winterthur Museum. Henry and his wife opened it to the public in 1951.

Winterthur is a unique assemblage of collections of period furniture, some two hundred room settings and 83,000 separate objects, mostly connected to history along the Eastern seaboard. The grounds are a gardening horticultural panoply, a laboratory for Henry, who was a horticulture student. Fortunately, there are guides and there is a tram for the grounds. It is a place you can get lost--literally lost. Along the Brandywine, if I can even say which state I'm in it's a lucky guess.

Nemours: The name for this spectacular country estate was adopted from the site of the du Pont ancestral home in north-central France. It is most fitting for the showplace home developed by Alfred I. du Pont. French-styled formal gardens surrounded by natural woodlands. Three hundred acres of Brandywine greenery frame this family namesake.

The mansion, a fine example of a modified Louis XVI French

chateau, was designed by Carrere and Hastings, and built in 1909 by Smyth and Son of Wilmington. Containing one hundred and two rooms, the house is furnished with fine examples of antique furniture, rare rugs, tapestries and outstanding works of art.

Also on this land is the Alfred I. du Pont Institute, a unique and important hospital, just for children. Since 1940 it has provided hope for acutely ill youngsters and anxiety relief for their parents.

Nemours, Longwood and Winterthur should be a visitor's first priority. But also allow time to visit the Hagley Museum, Rockwood, Brandywine River Museum, and there are still more.

Sleep in Style

The du Ponts built a hotel in Wilmington to match the caliber of their business clientele. It's the ultimate and you will be welcome. This company may have pioneered synthetics, but you'll find none in the Hotel du Pont. When your room receives a fruit plate with wine and the bed is turned back with chocolate for sweet dreams, you know you've risen above a plastic over-nightery. In the bath, brass fixtures sparkle. You'll find scales, robes, magnifying shaving mirror and towels that are big enough. The dining room table has a silver coffee server, a crystal bud vase. Overhead are bronze chandeliers and the Wyeth painting above your table is not a copy. (Toll-free number is in the Appendix.)

Before leaving the du Ponts, I need to salute one who did it *her* way. While most members of the family were busy preserving the status quo, one maverick wandered far afield and, like Martin Luther, nailed her Unitarian convictions to the meeting house door. Miss Zara, Coleman du Pont's sister, marched to a different drummer, 180 degrees off the du Pont course. Out of step, but never out of courage, she was just as determined to support her causes as the rest of the family was to build empires. "Aunt Zady" went to battle against social injustice with a passion. Pierre would have applauded her "fight for the public good." Aunt Zady believed in lots of "rights": *worker's* rights and *women's* right to vote and right to birth control. Years ahead of her time, she picketed and braved the paddy wagon. She never married, yet she raised a dozen du Pont offspring.

On May 2, 1946, the New York Times headlined her death:

MISS ZARA DU PONT, CHAMPION OF LABOR

" . . . until in her seventies she appeared on picket lines an average of three or four times a year . . . was a dues-paying member of sixty-three educational and progressive organizations, and contributed from her modest income to causes which she considered aimed at eradicating the sources of human ills . . . . "

Does anyone question that Zara du Pont didn't leave a monument? She *WAS* a monument.

11

The Empire State Building
Elevate Your Horizon—Start with a Skyscraper

Peerless—and a dozen other adjectives! This magnificent structure, launched at the start of the Great Depression, was a beacon of hope at a time when the country's morale was dragging bottom. Its mast, 1250 feet above the street below, sent out signals of hope to a city and a nation hard put to believe there was a future.

By recent standards it was a bargain. Its 40 million dollars bought a record-breaker in height, style and quality. Today that sum buys only a Van Gogh painting or a Beverly Hills rooming house. Now there are taller skyscrapers manyfold more costly, but there are none so classic in design, so ageless, and none that symbolize the national muscle like the Empire State Building. No other monument in our land boasts such a royal guest list. Its history is legend, its silhouette distinguishable among any grouping of skyscrapers. It has visibility. It says "New York."

What a team of planners and financiers! Pierre S. du Pont and John J. Raskob (the geniuses behind General Motors), Coleman du Pont (of the chemical empire), Louis G. Kaufman and Ellis P. Earle (New York real estate barons), all led by Alfred E. Smith, the four-time governor of New York State (whose yearly salary for running the show was $50,000).

A lucky combination of brains and experience made it happen: William F. Lamb, architect, H.G. Balcom, engineer, and Col. W.A. Starrett, builder. This powerhouse began site preparation in October of 1929, and on May 1, 1931, President Hoover pressed a button in Washington, D.C., officially recognizing this crown jewel in the Manhattan skyline.

Who in the 1990's can believe that in an era before computers and copy machines and lazer beams, a world-class skyscraper could be constructed in the heart of a busy metropolis in fourteen short—years? NO—months! That's a fact. Depression-hungry, dedicated craftsmen completed an art deco monument in less time than it would now take to get the environmental impact report. Fourteen months! And would you believe the construction of the Empire State Building came in twenty percent under budget?

Helen Keller describes her feeling after visiting the Tower her eyes could not see:

> "Standing there 'twixt earth and sky, I saw a romantic edifice wrought by human brains and hands that is to the burning eye of the sun a rival luminary. I saw it stand erect and serene in the midst of storm and tumult of elemental commotion. I heard the hammer of Thor ring when the shaft began to rise upward. I saw the unconquerable steel, the flash of testing flames, the swordlike rivets. I heard the steel drills in pandemonium. I saw countless skilled workers welding together that mighty symmetry. I looked upon the marvel of frail yet indomitable hands that lifted the Tower to its dominating height.
>
> Let cynics and supersensitive souls say what they will about American materialism and machine civilization. Beneath the surface are poetry, mysticism and inspiration that the Empire Building somehow symbolizes. In that giant shaft I see a groping toward beauty and spiritual vision."

What Helen Keller could not see, she felt. Like her, there's much your senses can add to this experience. Here you stand astride the location of the historic Astor House and the original Waldorf-Astoria Hotel. Yours is an experience none of those early-day bigwigs could savor. As they paraded along this Fifth Avenue block between 33rd and 34th Streets, their horizons were limited to a few blocks. But from your vantage you can see forever—across the Hudson to New Jersey you see the lower tip of Manhattan, Brooklyn, the Bronx and a sea of competing skyscrapers. Look down from your thousand-foot-high perch and relish this bird's eye view of the traffic you have escaped. Exciting! If the visibility is good you may be loath to leave. I always am.

Visitors are welcome and provided for. A ticket to the Observation Tower pays for your elevator ride round-trip. (You wouldn't like a 102-floor walk-up, would you?)

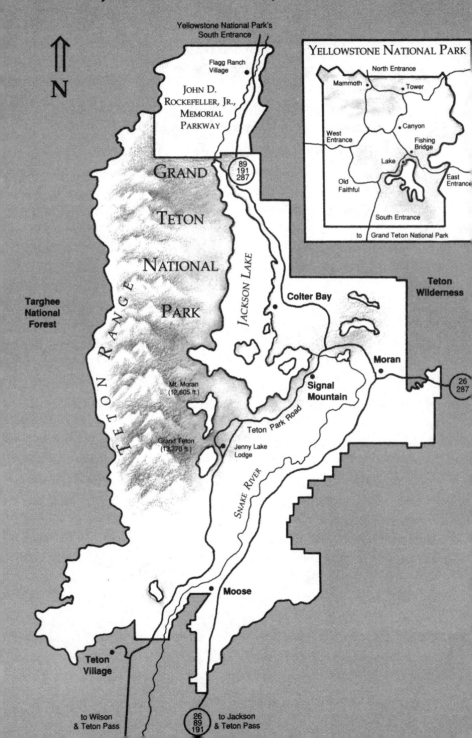

GRAND TETON NATIONAL PARK
AND THE JOHN D. ROCKEFELLER, JR., MEMORIAL PARKWAY

Yellowstone National Park's
South Entrance

Flagg Ranch
Village

JOHN D.
ROCKEFELLER, JR.,
MEMORIAL
PARKWAY

89
191
287

GRAND

TETON

NATIONAL

PARK

Targhee
National
Forest

JACKSON LAKE

TETON RANGE

Colter Bay

Teton
Wilderness

Moran

Signal
Mountain

26
287

Mt. Moran
(12,605 ft.)

Teton Park Road

Grand Teton
(13,770 ft.)

Jenny Lake
Lodge

SNAKE RIVER

Moose

Teton
Village

to Wilson
& Teton Pass

26
89
191

to Jackson
& Teton Pass

YELLOWSTONE NATIONAL PARK

North Entrance

Mammoth

Tower

West
Entrance

Canyon

Fishing
Bridge

Lake

East
Entrance

Old
Faithful

South Entrance

to   Grand Teton National Park

The Rockefeller Legacies

*"Go to almost any part of the earth and you find
Rockefeller money beneficently at work. The Rockefeller
family's philanthropies have done more than any other
single development to dispel the notion that all multi-
millionaires must necessarily be selfish mercenaries, bent
only on piling their fortunes higher and higher and crush-
ing the people lower and lower. Quite as great pains are
being taken to distribute worthily the Rockefeller millions as were taken to earn them."*

Forbes Magazine (10/15/29)

For over a century, Rockefeller wealth has covered the globe like
manna from heaven. To focus on just a few of its monuments called
for difficult choices. I selected my personal favorites from among a
vast assortment. For starters, here is a sketchy list of Rockefeller
benevolences which consumed a billion dollars.

If wonders of nature are important to you, consider some of
these real estate conservation efforts by Rockefeller money and altru-
ism:

Acadia National Park—In this area JDR, Jr. had a summer
home, along with many other notable and affluent neighbors. They
wished to conserve its pristine appeal, so around 1916, Junior bought
up thousands of acres of picturesque Mount Desert Island and gave it
to the Federal Government. Acadia became the first national park in
the east.

Grand Teton National Park—Here, in the northwest corner
of Wyoming, is a wilderness jewel. It is guarded on the west by the
Teton Range, a lineup of sharp peaks. They are majestic ghosts,
awesome as the Dolomites. In the mid-twenties, JDR, Jr. perceived
that this priceless region must be saved from exploitation. On the sly

he bought key parcels of what the locals called "The Jackson Hole," and then offered it to the Federal Government as an outright gift! Did the feds grab at this $13 million love offering? Not for twenty years! Thank God there was a rich far—sighted citizen willing to swallow the carrying costs for two decades while our politically hog-tied congress scratched its head. Anyone other than the likes of JDR, Jr. might have given up in disgust, and this national treasure would now be littered with billboards and road stands. Come 1972, the government got around to saying thanks. It named the scenic, eighty-two-mile corridor linking Yellowstone Park to Grand Teton Park the "John D. Rockefeller, Jr. Memorial Parkway." Amen! It was about time!

California Redwoods—This state is blessed with numerous environmental-ecology-focused movements such as the Sierra Club and Save-the-Redwoods League. The support they didn't get from then Governor Reagan ("If you've seen one redwood you've seen them all") was atoned for by the $2 million that came from J.D. Junior and resulted, over a protracted period, in Redwood National Park. Additional Rockefeller grants bought a whole forest that now guards the entrance to Yosemite.

Shenandoah National Park and the Blue Ridge Parkway—Follow the Appalachian Mountain crest along the western borders of Virginia and North Carolina all the way to the Great Smoky Mountains National Park of eastern Tennessee. All Rockefeller blessed.

The Palisades along the Hudson—Numerous gifts totaling millions of dollars preserved for the public this vulnerable Hudson riverfront from Fort Lee, New Jersey, to the New York border. Many public-spirited persons joined hands on this one, but without the $15 million from Rockefeller this fourteen-mile parkway might now be a riverfront industrial junkyard. Across from the Palisades is Fort Tryon and The Cloisters—another Rockefeller legacy, of course.

Even *Mesa Verde National Park*! How did Junior ever find this one at the remote southwest corner of Colorado? It was so isolated even the Native Americans were lucky to find their home in their cliff dwellings.

One could believe the Rockefellers were in a matching-grant game with the mighty federal treasury. Most of the foregoing gifts were conservation-motivated, and succeeded because the family and its many foundations could act promptly to buy time for our ponderous political system.

Colonial Williamsburg: perhaps the best-known and the most-visited Rockefeller gift to the public is, a short distance east of Richmond, Virginia. It's a salute to our founding fathers, to democracy and patriotism. John D., Jr. gave this one a lot of personal attention over several decades. Since his death, his sons, especially Winthrop, have carried on. The layout totals over $55 million. It is a showcase for visiting heads of state, a meeting place for global conferences, a trophy of American history. However, it is not necessary to be a history buff to enjoy the colonial capitol of Virginia.

The Visitor Center is your gateway to the city.

This is where you can buy your admission ticket and make reservations for dining, evening events and special programs. With your ticket purchase you'll also receive the "Visitor's Companion," your detailed guide to all events offered each week.

And this is where *Williamsburg—The Story of a Patriot* is shown—a dramatic 37-minute film that will help set the stage for your adventure. Simply show your admission ticket for entry.

Your admission ticket also allows you to use official Colonial Williamsburg transportation. Park for free, depart from the Visitor Center, and ride to points throughout the Historic Area.

In this beautifully restored colonial town, you'll get a feeling for the people and events that shaped colonial America. You'll walk the same streets George Washington and Thomas Jefferson did, and see where Patrick Henry made his impassioned plea for independence. The spirit of Williamsburg helped Virginia foster some smart philosophy.

But you can't get the full flavor of old Williamsburg simply by strolling down these pleasant streets or lanes. The 18th century comes most vividly alive when you enter the many homes, shops and public buildings.

Watch the sparks fly as the blacksmith shapes intricate hand tools. See the magnificent gun collection in the Governor's Palace foyer. Engage in a rousing debate with Master Hubbard about his colonial law practice. And gain an understanding of the people who lived and worked here as you tour the beautifully restored buildings furnished in authentic colonial style.

Heading north: Most New Yorkers—as well as people everywhere in the USA, including myself—sort of consider Rockefeller Center another legacy—or we did until recently. That's when the news broke that Mitsubishi had bought a 52% controlling interest. "Not Rockefeller Center!" we cried. Of all places! Many of us wondered, "Why?" Folks who've never left Pigeon Forge or Calabasas were shocked.

Perhaps the answer is that for years, we—the USA—have been on a shopping binge. In Japan! We've created a massive imbalance of trade, and the Japanese have a gigantic stockpile of our money. When a Van Gogh goes up for auction, they can bid eight-trillion yen. Some they convert to our choice real estate; and where is there any choicer property than the center of our big cities?

Well, Mitsubishi freed up $846 million for the Rockefeller clan. By nature the Rockefellers have been a philanthropic bunch, so I'm guessing some of it will trickle back down to me. Or maybe my grandkids. And, come Christmas, I'm betting the tree will be there and the skaters will be smiling. (And they'll be in New York City, not Tokyo.)

So I guess I'll accept the Japanese hospitality here in mid-Manhattan, and include it in my travel story. Especially because high up in one of its buildings is the fountainhead-quarters for many of the Rockefeller foundations. And also because of Radio City Music Hall, home stage for the world's top precision dance team. The Rockettes have delighted millions of theater-goers and sent them on with a quicker step. Each fourth Thursday in November, I can tune in the Macy Parade and my T-Day takes on added zest because of that phalanx of beautiful dancers. Thanksgiving for the Memories!

JDR Senior lived for nearly a century. He needed that longevity to orchestrate the innumerable grants his vast fortune made possible. His only son, JDR Junior, amplified his father's impact over a second lifespan, and instilled the same dedication into his five sons, who made their own headlines. JDR's youngest grandson is my age. Had I been a son of JDR Junior and been granted a wish, I would have asked to be the emissary in the creation of two great Manhattan shrines: St. John the Divine and Riverside Church. Then I could tell my grandchildren that I helped build a great gothic cathedral.

Ah—Riverside Church! Here my dreaming could ring the bells of the Laura Spelman Rockefeller carillon. I would walk beneath the saintly statuary of eighty of history's noblest. My entreaties would be spoken from the limestone pulpit sculpted from figures of twenty prophets!

The Cloisters: a few miles further north, along the Hudson River, is a branch of the Metropolitan. In this Museum of Medieval Art, one man's money and several men's ideas merged to become a trip to feudal Europe.

George Gray Barnard was an American romantic and sculptor of some note. He assembled elements of several medieval cloisters, shipped the entire collection to New York, and opened what he called his "cloister museum" on Fort Washington Avenue, just south of what is today Fort Tryon Park. The public reaction was enthusiastic, and one of Barnard's most prestigious visitors was John D. Rockefeller, Jr.

In 1925, Barnard offered his collection to the Metropolitan Museum, and Mr. Rockefeller provided funds for the purchase. The following year, enriched with art from JDR's personal collection, the museum opened as a branch of the Metropolitan. Sadly, Barnard died in 1938, shortly before its opening.

The land the museum occupied (also seven hundred acres across the Hudson) was purchased by JDR Junior to preserve the view.

The first director of The Cloisters, James Rorimer, describes the museum: " . . . not copied from any single medieval building, nor is it a composite of various buildings. The plan . . . was developed around architectural elements, dating from the twelfth to the fifteenth centuries, from the cloisters of five French monasteries."

Tireless attention to detail—including driveway entrances of Belgian blocks (formerly used to pave New York streets) which suggest old Europe—is obvious everywhere. The museum is wonderfully evocative of the Middle Ages. One of its best-known treasures is the series of seven tapestries: *The Hunt of the Unicorn,* woven near the end of the fifteenth century. These tapestries depict the chase, capture and death of the unicorn. Set in colors of unsurpassed brilliance, gardens and animals and people come superbly alive. The pheasant on the fountain admires his reflected beauty, the stag daydreams by the stream. The legend of the unicorn describes this symbol of the Middle Ages as cloven-hoofed, bearded like a goat, with an exquisitely long, fluted horn at the center of the forehead; too swift for even the greatest hunter to bring down. Capture required a beautiful maiden decoy deep in a forest where, in time, the unicorn would come to her, lay its head upon her lap and fall into a deep sleep. Then the hunters could pounce. To the medieval mind this capture symbolized, among other things, the betrayal of Christ.

A daily reminder of my visit to this extraordinary medieval museum hangs in our living room. You see, my wife is hooked on unicorns, and she did a skillfully-crafted needlepoint copy of "The Unicorn in Captivity."

"Cloister" means secluded. Tarry here awhile and meditate before you brave the pressures of the outside world.

Rockefeller family legacies are varied and rich. If the foregoing nominees don't meet your travel needs, go abroad. The family approach was international. Visit some of the restored antiquities of Europe, such as the Rheims Cathedral or the Palace of Versailles, and you will again be enjoying the Rockefeller largesse. It's worldwide. Be grateful and enjoy it!

The Breakers, Photo courtesy of
The Preservation Society of Newport County

Newport Mansions

This nineteenth-century showcase of conspicuous consumption! The epitome of a golden era of glitz! Extravagant, opulent, wasteful, profligate! Also wonderful, magnificent, mind-boggling, exquisite!

Why Newport, Rhode Island? Was it just a fateful happenstance? Well, Newport was a harbor in an age when most commerce moved by ship. In fact, the du Pont entourage of thirteen immigrants landed there on New Year's Day, 1800. Rhode Island had a tolerance for religious dissent, apathy about slavery, and was enterprise-friendly. It has a pleasant climate in summer, an absence of pesty bugs (more than Florida could claim), a charming coastline, an exciting ocean view, seclusion—a lot of things the rich like.

For whatever reason, Newport offered conditions right for the confluence of summer cottage enthusiasts. Cottages! Eight have been gathered into public domain by the Preservation Society of Newport County. We owe this group more than I can wrap in words. And, with painful reluctance, I must credit another force: the income tax. Our Internal Revenue Service offered, until recently, a strong philanthropy incentive for holders of property too large to manage. Entities such as the Preservation Society provided the conduit.

Where to begin? Bellevue Avenue. It is the hub of the Newport universe. It was a dirt road along which a southerner named George Jones decided, in about 1839, to build a home. It was quite advanced for its time, with water closets and bath inside—a bold breakthrough. He also wanted architecture! Gothic revival, no less. In 1863, Jones' cottage was acquired by William H. King for $35,000. It passed along to David King, Jr. In 1880, it was officially christened "Kingscote." Later, Stanford White, a famous architect, spruced it up and made it worthy of the mansion club. It came to the Preservation Society via King's second wife, Ella Louise Rives, of Virginia and Newport. She died in 1972 and willed Kingscote, its furnishings, and a trust fund for its maintenance to the Society.

Chateau-sur-Mer: Here is a Victorian creation built in two stages during the 1850s and 1870s, which bridged the transition from Kingscote (which is believable) to Marble House (which isn't). William Shepard Wetmore had it built in 1852, and died ten years after moving in.

His son, George Peabody, became master of Newport's most substantial dwelling when only sixteen years of age. He knew where he was going. After obtaining a law degree from Yale, he commissioned the best architect around, Richard Morris Hunt, to turn Chateau-sur-Mer into a fitting dwelling for his new bride: Edith Keteltas, a Newport lady. The year was 1869, and the newlyweds honeymooned in Europe during the time Morris was upgrading their home. It took a decade before George and Edith Wetmore settled into something suitable for a husband destined to be Governor of Rhode Island (two terms) and U.S. Senator (three terms). The Senator died in 1921, his wife in 1927. Their two daughters then basked in the social stratum of Newport, living in the Chateau until their lives ended. The Society acquired this splendid mansion in 1968.

The Elms: A victorian cottage purchased by Edward J. Berwind, a coal magnate, in 1888. Ten years later he had it "mansionized" to a French neoclassic that stretches the imagination. The money came right out of Appalachia and, if the coal miners in the Matewan movie could have guessed at the interior of this spread, there would have been rioting much sooner in West Virginia. It was the only Newport mansion where three carriages could be brought to the door simultaneously. It's a "gee-whiz" extravaganza with marble and crystal and wrought iron and stained glass and rare art and statuary and other unbelievables.

Mr. Berwind's wife, Herminie, preceded him in death by fourteen years. During this time, his sister, Julia, lived in the mansion with him and acted as hostess for the parties. Edward died in 1936 at age eighty-eight, and Julia summered in the cottage until 1961, when she died at age ninety-one. A year later the wrecking ball was at the door when the Preservation Society raised the $75,000 necessary to save it.

Rosecliff: For New York's socially elite, summering in Newport was the indispensable credential. It meant party invitation marathons, fun and games, dress to kill—and, to keep pace, one must have one's own mansion. Theresa Fair, the gold-miner's daughter, crashed the social register by marrying Hermann Oelrichs in 1890. However, Tessie was no carpetbagger. You will hear more about her in the chapter about the Fairmont Hotel. She had a pipeline into the Comstock Lode, thanks to her daddy who gave her $1 million for a wedding present. Hermann was only the heir to the German Lloyd Shipping Company.

The couple located a suitable piece of Newport dirt—eleven acres—a short drive off Bellevue. Ocean bluff frontage and lots of roses. Rosecliff! In 1891 it was overpriced at $140,000, but what's money when you've just inherited your mommy's share of the mine it comes from? Tessie hired the best architect available, Stanley White (Richard Morris Hunt being Vanderbilt-involved), and three years later, as if by magic, there was a summer cottage for the   Oelrichs.

Rosecliff is modeled after the Grand Trianon. French, of course—and big, of course. Certainly adequate for a couple with one child. My entire house would fit into its living room. No need for me to describe it, because you can see it in the movie, "The Great Gatsby," filmed in 1974. Robert Redford never had a stage prop to match it, before or since.

Tessie's reign came to an end, as happens with mortals. She died in 1926. Son Hermann occupied the mansion until 1941, and then sold it for $21,000. Seems incredibly cheap for a house that cost millions, but keep in mind that those same depression-era dollars could buy a decent apartment building or ten tract houses. The buyer, Anita Niesen, gave Rosecliff to her daughter, Gertrude. Someone forgot about plumbing in an empty house in winter. Burst water pipes flooded the structure.

Ray Alan Van Clief bought Rosecliff, had it repaired, had his staff of servants in place, and never saw his refurbished palace—he was killed in an auto accident en route to his own house warming.

The next owners had better luck. J. Edgar Monroe and his wife, Louise Stringer, purchased Rosecliff and brought it back to life. An infusion of Louisiana money for twenty-four summers brought with it parties and dinners, with hundreds of guests. In 1971 the Monroes gave their cottage and a trust fund to the Preservation Society. Now we can all party there. Bring a brown bag. But eat outside—this is no place to be messy.

How about a mansion break? Give the eyes a chance to shrink back into their sockets. Green Animals is a change of pace. It's a topiary garden. (Topiary means getting growing things to form into geometric patterns or animal shapes. Very popular in Europe way back in the 17th century.) Ten miles north of Newport, at Portsmouth along Narragansett Bay, are seven acres of garden. Sixty topiaries, 200 species of flowers. Really beautiful!

Thomas Brayton started these gardens in 1872. His daughter, Alice, carried on after his death in 1939. She died in 1974 at age ninety-four. Her will stipulated that Green Animals be a public legacy. The Preservation Society opens the garden, weather permitting, for a somewhat restricted season.

Richard Morris Hunt: Architect extraordinaire! You read about him in the chapter on the Biltmore Estate. For the latter part of his life, he was a Vanderbilt accessory. Talented, imaginative, rich, subservient, and inseparable from this story, he joined the Vanderbilts in pursuing their mansion competition. The next two creations are his masterpieces—both blue-ribbon winners.

Marble House was completed in 1892. In the Newport cottage game, it raised the ante to $4 million (plus $7 million for furnishings, I am told but unable to believe). It is guess-work to convert 1890s money into the century-later equivalent. There is an index for building costs. It computes to a multiplier of fifty to find the 1990s cost equivalent. Perhaps the present-day cost is pointless because they just don't build 'em that way anymore. The craftsmen would be nearly impossible to locate, and to accumulate such a sum of money before taxes—for a summer place! It's history.

Welcome to the house of William Kissam and Alva Smith Vanderbilt! The third-generation Vanderbilts are the focus in this book's drama. The family tree, included in chapter seven, will help you sort out the lineage and trace the money.

Mrs. William K. was coming upon her thirty-ninth birthday, and her husband wanted to give her something she didn't already have. Something really nice! And here I was—standing in it. This man, who was running his granddaddy's railroad empire, had standards to live up to and a $65 million inheritance to dispose of. (The rapid disposition of money was a third-generation specialty.)

Hunt was told to design the very best that money could buy. This opened a lot of options that few home owners have ever enjoyed. Marble of several varieties was brought from Europe—so much marble that it required its own wharf and warehouse on Newport Harbor. A regiment of Italian stonecutters shaped the marble. A steel entrance grille sixteen feet high between Corinthian pilasters seemed right. Enormous doors of gunmetal-finished steel over thick glass, one and a half tons each, were too heavy to be borne on hinges; they required pivots.

For intimate entertaining, Alva and William had a Louis XIV wood dining table just right for twenty or so. The solid bronze chairs around the table were too heavy for a guest to move alone—a footman was required on each side to do the positioning.

The dining room is a copy of the Salon of Hercules at Versailles. It has a large oil portrait of Louis XIV. The gilded ceiling reliefs of boars' heads, stag antlers, and fishing nets depict the King's favorite pastimes at Versailles. In the central ceiling painting, Hermes leads a goddess to Mount Olympus. (Had Hermes known of this place, he might have switched destinations.)

From room to room my guide piled adjective atop adjective. It was too much for my brain to process. My eyes glazed over. "Hal, you're not ready for this," I told myself. "Your carriage in the parking lot has Ford on its hood/bonnet. Your baronial villa last night was a bed-and-breakfast. You didn't attend France's Ecole des Beaux Arts; you passed art appreciation in school, but . . . . "

Alva Smith Vanderbilt is oft quoted for advising: "Marry twice—first for money, second for love." Her birthday present didn't do much for cementing the marriage. Only four years later she divorced William K., and soon thereafter married (for love) a friend of her ex, Oliver Hazard Perry Belmont. Her new husband had his own cottage down the street a bit. Belcourt Mansion was another Hunt creation. The ground floor was a multi-million-dollar stable. Belmont's horses kept up with the Astors. The gracious living was a floor above. It was Alva's wedding present, and she moved right in and enlarged it—but kept Marble House open because it had a better laundry.

Alva changed. Social causes, especially equal treatment for women, became her quest. Still, for a lady who was becoming increasingly critical of men, she was the beneficiary of some lavish male attention. When her antics drove Oliver to an early grave (in 1908) at age fifty, she inherited his fortune. Mansion games were getting boring, except for a last hurrah at Marble House, a suffrage fund-raiser in 1909. Her future priority was the campaign for women's right to vote.

In 1932, Alva sold Marble House to Frederick H. Prince, a wealthy Boston financier, for $100,000. A year later Alva died in France. Her body was returned to New York for burial. A score of women's organizations escorted her coffin up Fifth Avenue, twenty-one years after she had been leader of the suffrage parade up the same avenue. A great lady, a flamboyant newsmaker! Gone from the front page.

The Prince family lived at Marble House for thirty summers. In 1963, Harold Vanderbilt, Alva's son, gave a gift in memory of his mother, which enabled the Preservation Society to buy the mansion from Prince. Later the Prince Trust donated the furnishings.

In 1976, Gertrude Vanderbilt, widow of Harold, donated his yachting memorabilia, and now there is a room that bears his name and celebrates a yachting career that won a tidal wave of trophies. They are wall-to-wall. Finally, here is a Vanderbilt I can identify with. Harold V. and I share the same given name; also bridge. I play at the game, he merely invented it! Furthermore, I've skippered a boat or two. My favorite was my fishing dory on Cook Inlet. Vanderbilt's

Vagrant, Enterprise and Ranger were faster, I know, but how many salmon could they deliver to the cannery?

The Breakers! The Newport pinnacle. Here we see what a pair of Sunday school teachers could do with Vanderbilt money. Cornelius-the-second met Alice Claypoole Gwynne when they were church-goers in the same New York Episcopal Church. Both genteel and community-oriented. They had seven children. As head of his father's railroad empire, Cornelius was expected to keep pace at Newport, and whatever his mansion, it must denote supremacy.

Architect Hunt, again called into service, was on the spot to match or exceed Marble House. He looked to the Genoa palaces of the 16th century for a theme and presto, a seventy-room "cottage" fit for a king . . . also a Queen, for Alice had already taken unto herself the title, in Manhattan, of "*The* Mrs. Vanderbilt."

The site is a parcel of land back from Bellevue Avenue on Ochre Point. Cornelius bought an exciting access to the ocean, plus elbow room enough. The visitor here first encounters a 30-foot-high wrought iron gateway topped with the acorn and oakleaf family symbol. A gravel drive (to me a welcome respite from California's pervasive asphalt) leads to the large porte-cochere of the west facade. To reach this entry you must pass a commanding European Beech tree. It must be much older than The Breakers and just as rare and special. I took its picture and expect it happens frequently. Here I am hyperventilating over a tree, and haven't even glimpsed the structure $5 million bought in 1895. (It is the center piece of the picture on the back cover.)

Like Marble House, the Breakers defies description. My adjectives fail me. To pretend I can describe this palace would be a fraud. I can say it has an enormous heating plant in a distant building, which is joined to the house by a tunnel, and is adequate to store hundreds of tons of coal. Makes it fireproof! That I can comprehend.

The Mrs. Vanderbilt died in 1934, at age eighty-nine, and left the Breakers to her daughter, Gladys, then married to Count Laszlo Szechenyl. In 1948, the Countess leased the Breakers to the Society for $1, and this opened it to the public. Gladys paid the expenses until her death in 1972, at which time the Society purchased it for

$375,000—a sum less than the bare land cost eighty years earlier.

The mansion banquet is easier to digest if the visitor takes a break between courses. Save some energy for the cliff walk overlooking the Atlantic Ocean and adjoining some of these mansions. It's a designated National Recreation Trail. You can see it on the back cover. (Caution: it is potentially dangerous in places.)

Newport has many other attractions. Since its history is steeped in seafare, consider a visit to the Naval War College Museum. It emphasizes the development of the torpedo (at nearby Goat Island) and it salutes a lot of historic ships and Navy brass.

If legendary top guns you need, cozy up for the night with an admiral. A pair of young entrepreneurs addicted to hard work offer three centrally located B&Bs: The Admiral Fitzroy, a one-time convent now modernized, even has an elevator; The Admiral Farragut (looks like it may have been a speakeasy in rowdier days); or the Admiral Benbow. They belong to the era of the mansions, but have a toll-free number (see the Appendix), which is the only thing the Astors and Vanderbilts lacked.

My favorite sideshow is the Tennis Hall of fame. Here, in the gold-and-glitter era, the "casino" was a center of social activity. The National Championships were played here from 1881, until moved to Forest Hills in 1915.

In the Hall of Fame there are a hundred or so enshrinees, including Maureen Connelly. Hers is a story of triumph and tragedy featured in the NBC TV docudrama "Little Mo." She was struck by a truck in her prime of life and later died of cancer. Pause at her showcase for inspiration, then turn to Bobby Riggs' for laughs. Both San Diego champs.

One room in the Hall is devoted to women in tennis. Alva OHP Belmont should relish that, in whatever heaven she's now campaigning.

Photo courtesy Isabella Stewart Gardner Museum

14

The Isabella Gardner Museum
Fenway Court

The unconventional Isabella Gardner set Boston on its ear when she arrived from New York as the bride of one of Boston's oldest and most revered families. Although she is usually characterized as eccentric, she would be better described as unconventional. What she did was not really shocking, it simply was not "done."

Belle Stewart, born 1840, got off to a good start in a family that could send her abroad to school. She had whatever it took to capture the heart of Jack Gardner, a well-to-do Boston merchant with Peabody lineage. He was a birthright member of Boston's top crust, and his new wife was welcomed with considerable curiosity and raised eyebrows.

This flaunter of conventions was a generous and intelligent hostess. She was vital, curious, quick-witted, willful, seductively charming and dramatic. Her enthusiasms ranged from Oriental philosophy to the Red Sox. A complex woman, her correspondence reveals her to be at times imperious and egocentric, but more frequently as principled, loyal, thoughtful, generous and compassionate. She may have been quick to seek center stage, but she was just as quick to give it up to anyone with a talent to amuse, entertain or instruct. At home, Isabella gave lavish and often outrageous parties. She and Jack championed writers and artists. Her friends included Henry James, Oliver Wendell Holmes and John Singer Sargent. She launched young and struggling artists who needed a wealthy and appreciative public. She was a presence in the world of music; the Boston Symphony played at her soirees, and its conductor would not begin a performance unless Mrs. Gardner had taken her seat.

When Jack Gardner died in 1898 in his early sixties, Mrs. Jack turned to complete the plans she and her husband had nurtured. Her inheritance was not great, but her resolve was. Mrs. Gardner shut off rooms in her Beacon Street house to cut down on fuel costs. She stopped throwing lavish parties.

Isabella bought a tract of land for her home and museum, and spent most of her time planning the three-story building. She lunched at the site, directing masons and steamfitters. She wanted the museum to be magnificent, top quality. It took three years to create Fenway Court.

Bernard Berenson called her "the Boston end of the Arabian Nights" and wrote to his wife Mary: "She is the one and only real potentate I have ever known. She lives at a rate and intensity and with a reality that makes other lives seem pale, thin and shadowy."

On New Year's Day 1903, the cream of Boston society was invited to the unveiling of her dream.

Imagine you are there, sitting in the Music Room. Surrounded by tropical gardens, surveyed from the top of the stairs by a sleekly-gowned hostess, the Boston Symphony opens the evening. Friends and critics have been welcomed and seated. The music ends, a mirrored door rolls back to reveal an Italianate courtyard under a glass roof three stories above. Thousands of candles illuminate marble columns and Venetian balconies draped with flowering vines. In the midst of this New England winter, murmuring fountains and the scent of tropical flowers welcome "Boston's Best" as they spill into the Gardner Creation. The opening was talk of the town for years—not all of it appreciative. Somehow that lavish lushness was not considered quite properly Bostonian. Isabella's spirit was a source of delight and censure in a city not known for such display.

Isabella Gardner had no doubts about what she wanted and cared little about what others thought. She once had an entire marble staircase rearranged to suit her change of mind. She tolerated neither knaves nor fools, and was a source of delight and refreshment to many who dared to admit it. She bathed in the pool at the base of the double stairway at the south end of the courtyard, and was known to receive close friends there on occasion. She was marvelously outrageous in a time when women were generally to be seen and not heard much above a whisper.

Today, within the walls of the Gardner Museum, a splendid collection of over 2,000 of the world's art treasures span 3,000 years. Mrs. Gardner did not collect randomly. Her already-discerning eye was further trained by Harvard Professor, Charles Elliot Norton, and by her protege, Bernard Berenson, who was to become one of the leading experts on Italian Renaissance art. With Berenson's help, she purchased *The Rape of Europa* by Titian, which Rubens thought was the greatest painting in the world (so great the master himself copied it). The first Matisse work sold to an American museum went to Fenway Court. Landscapes by Whistler, portraits by Degas, Manet, and Sargent (including two of Mrs. Gardner) and paintings by Raphael and della Francesca are just a few of the masterpieces to enjoy here.

Perhaps a letter Mrs. Gardner wrote to a friend, who had helped her with financial advice, best expresses the depth of her passion for what she created:

Dear Mr. [Edmund] Hill,

My position is not quite what you think. Years ago I decided that the greatest need in our country was art . . . So I determined to make it my life's work if I could. Therefore, ever since my parents died I have spent every cent I inherited (for that was my money) in bringing about the object of my life. So you see for my personal needs I cannot possibly sell any work of art. I economize because what I save goes to the upkeep of my project.

Forgive all of this.

I.S. Gardner

STOP THE PRESS! The Gardner Museum was victim of an unwelcome distinction headlined on international television, March 18, 1990: the heftiest theft ever, dollar-wise, when two armed robbers disguised as police were allowed entry. They stole eleven paintings by famous masters. The value should not be equated in dollars, but money is the way our society keeps score, so a quarter of a billion is the educated guess.

There are terrible gaps in the Dutch Room where two great Rembrandts used to hang—the *Storm on the Sea of Galilee* and the *Lady and Gentleman in Black*—and near the window where Vermeer's *The Concert* and Flinck's *Landscape with an Obelisk* were displayed. Downstairs in the Blue Room Manet's *Chez Tortoni* is missing. A Rembrandt etching, five Degas wash or charcoal drawings, and a Chinese bronze beaker were also taken. For everyone who loves and enjoys the Gardner Museum, it is as if there had been a death in the family.

Did these reprehensible thieves believe they could take stolen paintings, or the money it brings, with them when they die? If this stolen art cannot be viewed and shared, of what worth is it to the possessor? One is reminded of the story of the clergyman who sneaked away to play golf on Sunday. He made a hole-in-one. But to whom could he boast? It was God's way of punishing the rascal.

What fools these knaves be. Why did they not enter by daylight through the front door, as we all are welcome to do? There are 290 paintings there to be enjoyed with no loss of sleep. (And even more across the street at the Museum of Fine Arts. It's a double-dip for a single trip.)

The attractions in this book are a demonstration of the "possessor's" need to share the "possession." More rewarding than to steal from a public treasure house would be to add to it. It is what Isabella (Mrs. Jack) Gardner did. In her will she left Fenway Court to the public. Until her death in 1924, she stretched her money to enrich this museum . . . and you should stretch your itinerary to enjoy it. When you do, check to see if the stolen art is recovered. It's my bet these paintings will someday be back where they belong.

Boston is different. It has a university most any direction you point, but don't expect to recognize one if you succeed in finding it. This city happened before automobiles and my best driving advice is *don't*! Public transit is OK. Subways glide beneath the traffic. Taxis are reasonable, traffic-worn and used to being trapped.

Visit the Christian Science Center. It has a reflecting pool with more water than a California P.U.D. A stroll through the "mother church" is inspiring. There are frequent guided tours. Then step across to the publishing building—the muscle and heart of the Christian Science Monitor. The lobby will be full of exhibits and just past these is the famous *Mapparium*. Enter it and you are into a geography lesson you will never forget. (In a sequel to follow this book, this attraction will receive detailed coverage.)

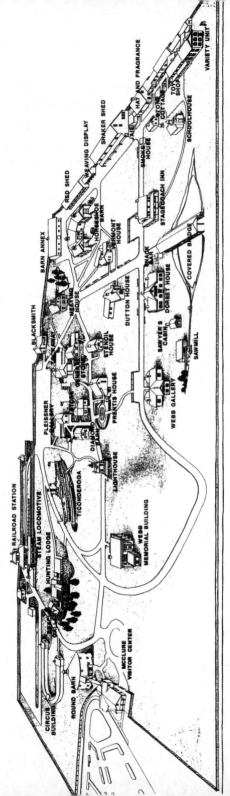

Shelburne Museum

Map courtesy of the Shelburne Museum, Vermont

15

Shelburne Museum

"If what I'm seeing is real, Robert Fulton would be proud," I told myself as I went for the brake pedal. Here on Route 7, approaching Burlington, Vermont, an apparition appeared. My eyes told me that off to the left, on a knoll miles from the lakefront, sat a big ship out of water. My logic told me that steamboats, even paddle-wheelers, don't crawl overland like toy windups.

Before I could unscramble this anomaly, I was staring at a string of livery horses trying to access the highway from a covered bridge. These steeds were traffic stoppers. I was lucky to hit the shoulder before causing an accident. I glanced back to see if my eyes had tricked me, then a quick turn around.

"Either Vermont harbors a practical joker, or somebody very rich collects crazy trophies," I thought as I backtracked to the entrance of the Shelburne Museum. *Museum*, I would soon conclude, is an insufficient label. It is more a potpourri of surprises, a kind of Vermont's "Believe It or Not." By sheer chance I had stumbled onto Electra Havemeyer Webb's legacy to the public.

In 1947, Mrs. Webb created this most unique place to house and share her vast collections of Americana with the public. She opened her attic to all of us and it's enough to drive a nostalgic wild. Set on forty-five scenic acres near Lake Champlain, the museum's thirty-seven buildings include an authentic one-room schoolhouse, six fully-furnished early New England homes, a jail, an Adirondack hunting lodge, a print shop and a lighthouse which once stood watch over Lake Champlain. We strolled through a transplanted covered bridge and boarded the S.S. Ticonderoga, a proud ship which once carried passengers across the waters of Lake Champlain.

Inside the museum's historic buildings, rooms are crowded with an eclectic mix of quilts, furniture, ceramics, dolls and toys, carriages, tools, carousel animals, the most extensive public collection of decoys in the world, weather vanes and whirligigs, scrimshaw and life-size cigar store figures. The Shelburne Museum also boasts an important collection of American and European art, including masterpieces by Andrew Wyeth, Grandma Moses, Ogden Pleissner, Rembrandt, Monet, Manet and Degas.

Permanent exhibits include "Vermont Farming Traditions" (displayed in a 1901 Round Barn) and the "Kirk Brothers Miniature Circus" featuring 5,000 hand-carved, painted circus figures. Working exhibits are featured in July and August and include printing, weaving and blacksmithing demonstrations. The Shelburne Museum has one of the finest lilac gardens in New England and a Lilac Festival is held each year in May. Other special events include "Grand Old Fourth of July" and a traditional "Early Vermont Christmas" the first weekend in December.

The museum grew out of Mrs. Webb's lifetime collecting propensity, with plenty of encouragement from her husband, J. Watson Webb. She was the daughter of "Sugar King" H.O. Havemeyer, who with his wife Louisine, started one of the earliest and finest collections of European Impressionist and Old Master paintings. Mrs. Webb inherited her parents' hobby, although her independent nature led her in very different aesthetic directions. Her mother was shocked when Electra, at age eighteen, brought home her first cigar store Indian.

The Shelburne Museum reflects Mrs. Webb's enthusiasm and her wish to share her things with the public. The museum is best seen as a "collection of collections," a very personal expression of one extraordinary woman's vision of American history and culture.

Mr. Webb had a Vanderbilt in his lineage, so the Museum hosts a railroad station, a steam locomotive and a private rail car. In 1890, Dr. W. Seward Webb (father of J. Watson) had the station constructed in Shelburne. Seward's father-in-law was the famous railroad magnate, William Henry Vanderbilt. Dr. Webb gave up his medical practice to immerse himself in railroading. His summer residence was a 4,000-acre estate near the town (see following attraction).

The private car, GRAND ISLE, has an illustrious history. It is an appropriate icon to the Vanderbilt era and a worthy companion to the Ticonderoga and the covered bridge. All symbols of travel in a bygone era: horse, paddle-wheeler and steam rail.

Back to that whale out of water, the Ticonderoga. It had me hooked. What made the Shelburne Museum folk, forty-five years ago, think they could possibly get a 900-ton ship moved two and a half miles over rough terrain to be put on display at their museum? The move required building a ship lock to give a twenty-five-foot lift to the terra firma shore. Parallel, level rail lines were required. A brook, a highway, a railroad and a swamp obstructed the route. Progress was measured in inches and feet in the middle of a Vermont winter!

Many winters I lived in interior Alaska. I know C-O-L-D! I remember that wet, frozen mittens and boots on slippery slopes don't shuck much corn. I would bet nine hundred tons of ice what they did was impossible! It couldn't happen! Except there it sits, a behemoth, a long way out of water.

The feat exemplifies legendary New England grit. See the free movie aboard the "Ti" that chronicles the story. You'll be moved just seeing it moved.

The Ticonderoga was a proud ship worthy of saving. It was built in 1906 at a Shelburne shipyard, just one hundred years after Fulton demonstrated the feasibility of steam. It was the twenty-ninth and last sidewheeler to ply the waters of Lake Champlain. She was a trim ship, 220 feet long, 59 feet wide, 892 tons of displacement, 18-foot paddles, three decks, twenty staterooms, a speed of 20 mph and a passenger capacity of over a thousand.

By 1954, the Shelburne Steamboat Company had dissolved and the museum, owner of all the stock, had this pet whale on its hands. The Webbs bit the bullet and spent $170,000 (that converts to $1,238,000 in 1990s money) to save it—more than it cost to build.

Across the continent is a California counterpart, a water creature also stranded high and dry, also 220 feet long but only one-fourth the weight: Howard Hughes' "Spruce Goose" at Long Beach (Chapter 30). The goose and the whale should be pen pals, each cradled out of its element and stared at by bug-eyed skeptics. Getting the Spruce Goose planted on land beside the Queen Mary (another stranded sea orphan) was a newsworthy feat, but it was accomplished with modern state-of-the-art equipment. To this writer, the Ticonderoga's flight from the wrecking ball tops all the other escapes!

J. Watson Webb, Jr. succeeded his mother as the museum's director. Today the museum continues to grow and develop. It is a non-profit educational institution and is supported principally by admissions, bequests and contributions. There is on-the-grounds jitney service, a cafeteria and ample free parking. Visitors get a "second consecutive day free" admission. Shelburne is only a few minutes south of the Burlington Airport.

When I visit this "Treasure Trove," I am seeing the story my grandparents tried to tell me when I was too busy to listen.

The Inn at Shelburne Farm

Now here's a surprise. Shelburne Museum has an in-law worthy of a visit. If you have followed the route this book takes, you have absorbed a bit of the Vanderbilt glitz. Quite a bit, in fact. Now you are in the right place to stay in a Vanderbilt mansion. Here on the shores of Lake Champlain is the home of Eliza ("Lila"), granddaughter of "the Commodore" and mother of J. Watson Webb.

In 1881, Lila married William Seward Webb, her father's henchman—today the job carries the title "CEO" with fifty times the money. Webb was destined to thrive in the railroad empire. Eliza's inheritance in 1885, a cool ten million, certainly enhanced the Webb financial statement. These young marrieds chose the Lake Champlain countryside for their starter home. No third-generation Vanderbilt could do anything small. The result was a sixty-room "cottage" on a thousand acres. You can sleep there if you wish and here's why:

the great-grandchildren cherished its import and opened it to the public.

The children of Derick Webb, grandson of William Seward, created a non-profit entity to which their father deeded the property: Shelburne Farms Resources. Its noble purpose is to ". . . teach and demonstrate the stewardship of natural and agricultural resources." An operating farm for teaching? Yes, and one on the cutting edge of the ecology-environmental movement.

Centerpiece of the farm is the largest barn ever built, as of 1888, and its two-acre courtyard. It housed forty teams of mules, workshops, storage for 2500 tons of hay. A visitor center is due to open in 1991. Visit there if you hanker to milk a cow, churn some butter, card wool, help bees build a honeycomb, smell the harvest, press apples for cider and get your hands in the soil. However, aren't you here to spend the night?

Shelburne Inn, the Vanderbilt-Webb family home, now caters to the public with a modified American Plan for travellers wishing to savor Queen Anne decor and lifestyle. Only twenty-four rooms are available. There are wonderful gardens (restored from Lila's journal), originally planned by Frederick Olmstead, the landscape architect who designed Central Park in New York City, parks all over Boston and the Biltmore Estate. On returning home, you can tease your friends with, "I overnighted (a) at a farm; (b) in a Vanderbilt mansion; (c) along Lake Champlain in the country; (d) all of the foregoing."

Roosevelt Home, Hyde Park, New York, exterior, front, Courtesy of Franklin D. Roosevelt Library

"He particularly admired the beautiful view, as did everyone, from the terrace at the southern end of the house. One stepped out long French windows from the living-room library and onto a green lawn. Many times in summer, when I would be told that 'the family was on the lawn,' I approached through the library and saw through the open door an unforgettable picture: Mrs. Sara Roosevelt, in a soft, light summery dress with ruffles, her hair charmingly curled, sitting in a wicker chair and reading; Mrs. Roosevelt, in a white dress and white tennis shoes with a velvet band around her head to keep her hair from blowing, sitting with her long-legged, graceful posture in a low chair and knitting, always knitting; Roosevelt looking off down the river at the view he admired, with a book, often unopened, in one hand, and a walking stick in the other; dogs playing near by, and children romping a little farther down the lawn. The scene was like a Currier and Ives print of Life along the Hudson.

- Frances Perkins in
The Roosevelt I Knew

16

Roosevelt Home
Hyde Park & FDR

If you are old enough to have felt the impact of the WPA or the NRA or the SEC or AAA or CCC, then Hyde Park is your nostalgia bin. If your resume dates you back to WWII, then come reminisce with Commander-in-Chief Roosevelt.

The year 1932 found our nation mired in a desolate depression. Banks were failing, bread lines lengthening, factories locking up, farms going on the block. It was a bad year for incumbents and a good year for charisma. Crisis time! There was no precedent to learn from, there was no safety net, there was no benevolent uncle. The USA was scraping bottom and didn't need to be told it was sick. We wanted desperately to hear that there was a way out. The American people elected Franklin Delano Roosevelt to lead them out of the wilderness. Their Moses was a turn-around innovator, a novelty in the White House.

It can be argued until doomsday whether Roosevelt did the right things, and nobody will contend that everything worked. No remembering person can deny that Roosevelt did "something," and when compared to the inaction of other administrations, he did "everything." His programs had the impact of a revolution.

No other president has won four elections. No other president has surmounted back-to-back crises of the magnitude of the Great Depression and World War II. No other president has battled such challenges while overcoming severe physical affliction and disguising it so effectively. Incredible!

Incredible, yes; but not surprising. He was a Roosevelt, he was a Delano, he grew up at Hyde Park. Not to succeed would have been the surprise.

To be a toddler at Hyde Park was to frolic in manna. To be the maturing son of James and Sara Roosevelt was a jump start. To have the Hyde Park address was an inside lane on the fast track. To grow to manhood along the Hudson was to rub elbows with the great, the near-great, and the soon-to-be-great.

The dialog could have run as follows:

"Mother, I want to go hang out at the neighbors . . . . "

"That's fine, Franklin, and if they're having guests just be polite—kings and queens and tycoons and ex-presidents and senators expect children to show respect. Also be careful around their European art and statuary. Oh, and if Fred Vanderbilt is there, tell him his cows are in our woods . . . . "

To finesse FDR's opponents, if he had any, he need only sortie down the road a few miles to the Beekman Arms Inn where the stagecoaches between Albany and New York City changed horses. Here he could learn the news and gossip before the newspapers had it. Here he could soak up the aura of Horace Greeley and William Jennings Bryan and governors and presidents. (Here he might have surmised he would someday give informal talks after campaigns for governor and president—which he was sure to win.)

The average American politician follows a well-trod path to elective office. He strikes deep roots in a likely community—joins countless organizations, is active in the church, in charities, civic affairs. FDR did virtually none of these things. In 1910 he had not lived year round at Hyde Park since leaving for Groton fourteen years before. He stayed at his mother's house many weekends and summers, but saw little of the townspeople.

At party functions, Dutchess County Democrats looked over the young man and had mixed feelings about him. His patrician and somewhat supercilious bearing and speech, his slight acquaintance with the district, his youth and inexperience were a concern. On the other hand, he bore the magic name of Roosevelt. And he had money—money for his own campaign with enough left over for the party treasury.

To test the water, FDR ran for state senate. He was twenty-nine, the son of a Democrat, living in a county that had gone solidly Republican for thirty-two years. It was his first try. Won by a landslide, of course.

In view of Roosevelt's electoral prowess, his vote-getting record in Hyde Park and Dutchess County is a surprise. In his long political career, FDR contested nine general elections--two for state senator in 1910 and 1912, one for vice president in 1920, two for governor of New York State, and four for president. He carried Hyde Park in only three of them—the two state senator races and his second run for the governorship in 1930. Otherwise, the closest he came to carrying Hyde Park was in the 1940 presidential election, when he received 48.9 percent of the vote against Wendell Willkie's 50.9 percent.

Early on, Roosevelt must have sensed impending greatness and power. The political and social environment in which he moved was charged with success. After all, he shared a legacy that propelled a cousin to the White House, had neighbors with power-names like Astor and Vanderbilt, he travelled extensively in Europe and was schooled there. His was a background that enabled him to assure a despairing nation: "We have nothing to fear but fear itself . . . " And the nation took heart.

Yet, a success-prone political and social environment cannot, by itself, propel a young man to the State Senate at age twenty-nine, to Assistant Secretary of the Navy at age thirty-one, to the governorship of New York after a crippling bout with infantile paralysis which left his legs useless, and ultimately to the very presidency. That requires more than neighbors who can kick open doors, it requires more than family connections, it requires more than luck. It requires genius, inner strength, an agile brain and astute timing. FDR had the right stuff!

Right stuff and the right genes. Above the fireplace in Hyde Park hang two portraits: a Gilbert Stuart painting of Isaac Roosevelt, FDR's great-grandfather, who was active in the Revolutionary War, a member of the State Constitutional Convention, a state senator, and a member of the state convention which ratified the Constitution of the United States. The other portrait is of Franklin's great-grandfather James Roosevelt, who was a New York City merchant, a state assemblyman, an alderman, and the first of the family to settle in Dutchess County in 1819.

It became a tradition of Hyde Parkers to march in a candle-light parade to Roosevelt's house in celebration of the latest victory. At the estate on election nights a stand-up dinner was customary before guests became absorbed with election returns. In a little room to the left of the front hall sat FDR's mother, Sara, with several old lady friends. A radio was on, but sewing, knitting and chatting were the major entertainment. In the big living room was another radio and a large gathering of guests. The President sat in the dining room with his sons and members of his staff. Large charts littered the dining table and news tickers clattered in the pantry. Mrs. Eleanor Roosevelt moved from one room to another seeing to the needs of the guests. Later, the President and all of his guests went out on the front porch to greet a parade of Hyde Park townspeople.

In time Roosevelt became aware that no private home could ever, or should ever, hold the many collections which came to him while in the presidency.

The war increased his awareness that things of historical interest should not all be concentrated in one place. Modern war could, with one bomb, destroy the Congressional Library, and FDR wanted his papers available to future historians. He decided to give a piece of land at Hyde Park for a library to be erected which would then be given to the government of the United States. When this was done, the family home was also deeded to the U.S.

Eleanor Roosevelt wrote in some personal recollections after the President's death:

"I think Franklin realized that the historic library, the house, and the peaceful resting place behind the high hedge, with flowers blooming around it, would perhaps mean something to the people of the United States. They would understand the rest and peace and strength which he had gained here and perhaps learn to come, and go away with some sense of healing and courage themselves. If this place serves this purpose, it will fulfill, I think, the desire which was nearest my husband's heart when he gave the place to the Government.

I am always glad that we were able to leave the rooms exactly as they had been, since my husband asked in his memorandum to me that we take out only what we could use and that we leave the house, if possible, looking 'lived in.'"

Lived in! Yes . . . but what an understatement. History was made in these rooms. The President's office was his "summer White House." Here, on June 20, 1942, the President and the British Prime Minister, Winston Churchill, signed the agreement that resulted in the world's first atomic bomb. It was from this room that FDR broadcast his last campaign speech preceding his fourth election as President. There is a mystical feeling one experiences in the Hyde Park home—the occupants are merely away and may return. They are away, but not far. Franklin and Eleanor Roosevelt are buried a few steps away in the beautiful and simple rose garden that was so cherished by his mother. No embellishments, no statuary, no glitter. Only two large granite markers to remind all who view them that our nation overcame two epic crises that spanned thirteen years under the leadership of the man who, undaunted despite a wheelchair, refused to be afraid of fear.

★ MUSEUM OF THE FRANKLIN D. ROOSEVELT LIBRARY ★

"We've got a New Deal for you."

NRA
MEMBER
U.S.
WE DO OUR PART

★   ★   ★   ★   ★   ★   ★   ★   ★   ★   ★   ★   ★

This is the mansion that Fred built,
This is the man who drew the plans
to create the house that Fred built.
This is the builder who read the plans
that were drawn by the clever architect man
to create the house that Fred built.
This is the one who designed the insides
of the mansion that Fred decreed to be built
by the builder who followed the beautiful plans
drawn by the architect, clever man—
all for the house that Fred built.
Here's the collector who found the furnishings—
Here are the artists who painted the pictures—
These are the gardeners tending the plantings
and
This is the maiden who married the man
whose name is George or Frederick Van
who built the mansions in this book.

Hyde Park Mansion
The Hyde Park Vanderbilts

Only twenty-two and Frederick William Vanderbilt wanted to marry. Chose a beautiful lady twelve years his senior. Her father was a wealthy New York financier. But! Louise Anthony Torrance was divorced and Daddy William Henry didn't go for that sort of thing. Which Frederick very well knew. So they got married on the sly, as couples in love sometimes do, and it was weeks before Daddy found out. The result was that Frederick came off with a skinny $10 million bequest when his father died seven years later.

This third son of William Henry, grandson of the Commodore, was in the only branch of the family tree to share the money—but not evenly (see the genealogy with Chapter seven).

To catch up with his older brothers' inheritances, Frederick had to dig in. Actually work! He got a job in the city running companies, making deals, stock options, golden parachutes, and ten years later was ready to compete with others in the mansion game. Frederick bought Hyde Park property. It was 1895; Franklin Roosevelt was thirteen and the news that a Vanderbilt was moving in shook up the neighborhood. And this one had a job. Ran a railroad. Several of them, in fact. Something outrageous, that's what he'd build. Vanderbilts always did.

Rumor was, Frederick Vanderbilt wanted a working farm! Call-of-the-soil stuff. Gentleman farmer, to be sure—and, since he was Dutch, probably a good one. Along the Hudson Frederick would be among his countrymen. The 600 acres he chose had come down through John Jacob Astor. About the right size for a $521,466 second home in the country (plus another $2 million for the grounds and outbuildings).

Architects McKim, Mead & White drew plans for about fifty Italian Renaissance rooms, on four levels. Just the basics for a couple

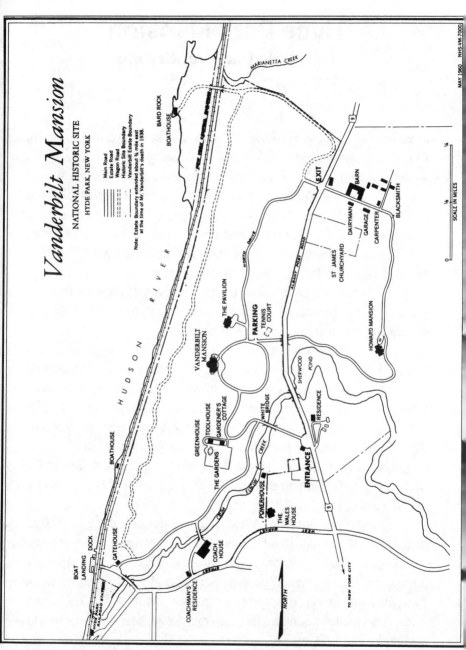

Map of Vanderbilt Estate, Hyde Park, New York

with no children. They built "The Pavilion" to live in during construction—a small Georgian colonial with only sixteen rooms and three baths—adequate for interim housing.

Having recently been in Newport, also Asheville, I am well qualified to describe *this* beauty. It's Italian Renaissance alright. Has a main hall with enough marble to pave a dozen driveways, a fire-place, tapestries with their coat of arms, and expensive accessories here and there. There's a study, a den, a drawing room (18th century French for sure), foyers, living room and space enough for guests waiting for dinner. Upstairs . . . but let's check out the farm before climbing the steps.

Yes, it was an operating farm. Some sixty full-time employees ran the estate. Of these, about twenty took care of the residences. The rest worked on the grounds and on the farm with hundreds of Jersey cattle, a dozen Belgian draft horses and an assortment of chickens and pigs. Animals were slaughtered and dressed, butter churned, eggs gathered; and enough vegetables grown to fill the tables at the manor house, the Manhattan townhouse, and for entertaining on the yacht moored down on the Hudson. Oh, yes! There were carriage horses too, which were moved regularly back and forth from country to city—on a special railroad car, of course.

It kept a country squire busy. Mr. V. must have been quite an organizer to manage railroads, estates, enjoy yachting, sojourns to Europe, bask during winter breaks at Palm Beach, check in at the Vanderbilt "cottage" for the Newport social season, fit in time at his Japanese retreat camp in the Adirondacks and even make runs to the West Coast (which took seven days in a private rail car). Did he ever sleep?

Which brings me up to the second floor of the mansion. The largest room overlooks the Hudson River and the mountains beyond. This splendid view occupied my interest while waiting for my niece who was inching her way up the grand stairway.

"Jo, here's a room with a special message," I teased. She was slow to catch on.

"Why? They're all special, all fifty of them. I can't be choosy. "

I persisted. "This is the Blue Room where Mrs. Vanderbilt's niece stayed when she visited her Aunt and Uncle. Mrs. Van Alen must have made the right moves because she inherited the whole spread. So you see, we uncles may be curmudgeons . . . but also a resource."

My niece nodded, gave the Van Alen bedroom a furtive glance, moved on to the marble balustrade. Jo's good company on a trip, and after Hyde Park even more so. Thereafter, an added delight was the wake-up knock on my door to admit my smiling niece with a breakfast tray, hot coffee, rolls, the paper and a clever quip.

Van Alen owned the Hyde Park estate but a short time, for when President Roosevelt told her he was giving his Hyde Park home to the Federal Government and suggested she might want to do the same, she did.

Vanderbilt Mansion National Historic Site is now administered by the National Park Service. Your Golden Age Pass admits you free. The Pavilion serves as Visitor Center, however it may not be open part of the winter. When you visit, set your imagination free. Let it turn back the clock to life in an earlier era. Stroll through the woods, ride to the hounds, sail on the Hudson in summer and ice-boat in winter. Sleigh-ride behind fast-stepping horses just as Vanderbilt did. Sing out as you glide over crisp packed snow, "Sleigh bells ring, are you listenin' . . . ." Oh, and as you sit in the evening with your back to a crackling fire in the huge fireplace, read by lantern light the poem that John Greenleaf Whittier wrote—*Snowbound*.

MILTON HERSHEY SCHOOL
HERSHEY, PENNSYLVANIA 17033

His deeds are his monument
His life is our inspiration

Hershey School & Hotel
The Chocolate Man
and His Ivy League Orphanage

Milton S. Hershey, the man whose name is synonymous with chocolate bars, was an industrialist and humanitarian of the first order. To the thousands of graduates of the school he founded in Hershey, Pennsylvania, he is the man who left them a living heritage.

Soon after launching the chocolate business for which he became nationally known, Milton Hershey established a school for youth in need. As his business grew, so grew the endowment that provided an education, a home and a way of life for children deprived of a normal family. Hershey made it possible for thousands of young people to have the opportunities to develop their creative abilities without cost to them.

In 1909, the school opened with four boys. Since that time the campus facilities have been expanded until today it accommodates 1,250 boys and girls. Bad luck helps a child to qualify, but thereafter, and until schooling is over, this institution is a good luck charm.

Foster parent Hershey can write a mighty big check. The voting shares and 42 percent of the equity in Hershey Foods is one sweet endowment, worth over $1 billion. Many Ivy League colleges would gladly trade places.

Milton Hershey School provides, through its elementary, intermediate and senior high programs, an educational opportunity for children whose natural family relationships have been disrupted. Student homes provide a warm family life, stabilizing discipline and the security youths need to use fully the educational advantages they receive.

How did a simple Pennsylvania Dutch farm boy from a broken home, forced to drop out of school in the fourth grade, go on to become one of the wealthiest and most famous men of his day? Is it possible to explain the mind of a youth drilled in the tenets of the Mennonite faith, who, as a forty-one-year-old bachelor, met and married Catherine Sweeney, a twenty-four-year-old Irish Catholic? How can anyone understand or interpret the inner thoughts of a man who never kept a diary, rarely wrote a letter, never made a speech and, aside from the Bible, may never have read a book in his life?

How indeed? Examining the biographies of the giants featured in this book, answers as to how and why are as varied as they are inexact. Most of them could not have succeeded without a special ingredient coupled with an oversized ego. Most built their monuments first, only later turning to endowments and philanthropies. Not Milton S. Hershey. He marched to a different drummer. As soon as he was out of debt, he turned his energies to his dream of a school for boys in need. He knew about need from his own boyhood. He knew about living poor. His experience grew into a dedication that matched his business success, and his two passions soared together. In time, most of his fortune was pledged to his philanthropy. Milton S. Hershey belongs in this book because of his unique and total commitment. Although I must admit a bias: I am a congenital chocoholic.

From my earliest youth, without the slightest inkling that my purchases were supporting an orphanage school, I was a patron of the Hershey candy bar. There was a time in my life when Hersheys consumed all of my pocket money. And there was a time when tinsel-wrapped Kisses were the most cherished of table decorations. For you food faddists who abstain from chocolate, I just want to assure you that a kid who was addicted to Hershey bars has survived into his seventies. Mr. Hershey lived to the respectable age of eighty-eight.

I visited my childhood spending money in Hershey. What a happy discovery! We chocoholics helped create a noble living monument! Its hub is Founders Hall, a landmark structure as visible and meaningful as the Chocolate Factory in the middle of town. It is a tribute to Milton and Catherine Hershey and an activity center for their school. The interior is sheathed in glistening Vermont marble. A vaulted dome displays the flags of the fifty states, recalling that students have come from across the nation. Set in the rotunda floor is a mosaic medallion depicting events in the life of the "founders." The Hall contains a chapel-auditorium (to seat 2,600) with stage lighting and equipment second to none in the nation. Founders Hall sparkles. It radiates a reverence rare to campuses. It is a must see!

Whatever you do in Derry Township, Pennsylvania, it will be Hershey-connected. You may wish to learn about chocolate from tropical plantation to delightful confections in "Chocolate World," where a circuitous tram takes you on an enlightening ride. Enjoy the rides and thrills of Hersheypark. Ice Capades? Hersheypark Arena. Broadway show? Hershey Community Theatre. Antique Car Show? Of course. It's all there, Hershey-style. Plus a memorable hotel—named "Hotel H-----y," of course!

You need not like chocolate to appreciate this delightful hotel, but if you do, the Kisses on your pillow will send you off to dreamland with a smile. Mr. Hershey determined to build this jewel during the great depression. Building it would provide employment for the community at a time of severe economic stress. (This man was a humanitarian.) He wanted Mediterranean styling, with spacious verandas and courts, indoor and outdoor swimming, and everything for gracious living. He wanted a prestigious hotel in keeping with his business success.

The formal dining room deserves special attention. When you dine there, enjoy the crystal, the silver, the carpet, the upholstered chair, art work, elegant surroundings. Thirteen famous stained-glass windows surround you with Pennsylvania flora and fauna. They are the work of J. Hourse Rudy, a skilled artist from York, and his team. Took a solid year to create.

After your meal, if it's still daylight, take a stroll through Hershey Gardens. It is a botanist's candy store. Twenty-three acres with too many species to name. Plus some funny statuary. It's but a short walk. It goes with the hospitality.

If a figurehead for the work-ethic ever deserved enshrining, it is certainly Milton S. Hershey. When he died in 1945, his endowment was firmly anchored to the soil from which he had sprung.

When the wind is right, I'm guessing the heavenly aroma of

chocolate scents the air breathed in nearby Harrisburg. Pennsylvania's capitol building deserves a visit. A Renaissance edifice with dome styled after Rome's St. Peter's Basilica, and staircase after Paris' Grand Opera House. Teddy Roosevelt dedicated it about 1906. Back then a body could take pole in hand and amble a few steps over to the Susquehanna and catch fish almost standing on the Capitol lawn. That's probably changed.

Photo courtesy of Hotel Hershey

*Photo courtesy of Heinz Hall for the Performing Arts,
Pittsburgh, Pennsylvania*

The Carnegie

Andrew Carnegie, pondering his money, at age sixty-seven:
"I knew the task of distribution before me
Would tax me in my old age to the utmost . . .
It's wrong to die with it."

Mention the name of this industrialist and try to describe in a single word his symbol: Railroads? Steel? Philanthropy? Libraries! Of course. And how about "Evangelist"! Here we have a much-in-demand speech-maker who went about the country proclaiming "The Gospel of Wealth"—how to acquire it and why to get rid of it.

In gospel circles, a preacher who can be billed as "converted sinner" somehow sounds more convincing. So what of a rich man who started poor as dirt and admonishes the rich to dispose of their wealth?

"The man who dies rich dies disgraced," Carnegie contended. Imagine a dedicated workaholic plugging for fortune-making and condemning keeping it; that's like catching fish and throwing them back. Because he spoke from experience, he was convincing.

Carnegie was steadfast and serious about making money. In the decades when he was building his steel-industry conglomerate, he condoned labor abuses and strife. In that era, it was how the game was played. Even so, he lived to regret this aspect of money making.

Near the end of the nineteenth century, Carnegie concluded enough was enough—and perhaps too much. He turned his energy to disposing of money and, in a way, redeemed the ugly episodes that had stained his escutcheon. By then his wealth had a present-day purchasing power of perhaps $10 billion. Try as he might, he was unable to dispense money as fast as it piled up. He wanted his giving to be prudent and effective—"Scientific Philanthropy" he called it.

More people than realize it have felt the Carnegie gospel. Church-goers of earlier times, who sang and enjoyed the music, may have been hearing one of 8,000 church organs donated by the Carnegie Fund. From the Grand Catholic Cathedral of Pittsburgh to small country churches, God has heard more melodious choruses because the humble, hard-working son of a Scottish weaver believed his great wealth should serve noble purposes.

Whether Carnegie believed that God dwelt on high is speculative, but he became engrossed in searching the heavens, and so underwrote Mount Wilson observatory in California, which has discovered a score of new worlds.

Carnegie pursued world peace and searched for world-class heroes. These he rewarded for their heroic deeds, and set up annuities for families of those who perished in efforts to serve their neighbors. Since 1904, over 1500 heroes have been honored and rewarded. The search for candidates is ongoing today.

Carnegie's success story is almost an argument in favor of child labor and self-education. Here was a lad born November 24, 1835, in Dunfermline, Scotland, as the eldest son of a weaver who brought his family to the new world for a better life. Relatives offered a sheltering place at Allegheny and thus did fate ordain Western Pennsylvania as young Andrew's training turf—and monument site.

Up the career ladder:
    Age 14—$1.20 per week winding bobbins. His first
        job and a dirty one
    Age 14½—$2.50 per week, delivering telegrams
        and making himself noticed; for example,
        sweeping the office on his own time
    Age 15—$11.25 per month—took on added re-
        sponsibility and learned telegraphy
    Age 16—$13.50 per month—expanded his territory,
        subbed out part of the delivery to his Scottish
        buddies, all of whom became rich

Age 17—$30 per month—in charge of the telegraph office

Age 20—$40 per month as dispatcher for a Division of Pennsylvania Railroad

Age 24—$1500 per year—superintendent of the Division

Forget the pay. Young Carnegie was learning. Learning that steel was the successor to iron and would be in great demand by the USA's emerging industrial power. He foresaw that wooden bridges would someday be replaced with steel; that steel was the keystone to future construction. It was a typical Carnegie move to form a steel company (Keystone Bridge), to find five partners to put up $1250 apiece, to implement a series of brilliant steel-improving formulas and furnaces. His steel company furnished the frames for the Brooklyn Bridge, the Washington Monument, elevated trains, skyscrapers. In time he sold the whole kaboodle to J.P. Morgan, and thirty of his associates became millionaires.

His next challenge was to dispose of the accumulation. Carnegie's "Gospel of Wealth" took shape through several magazine articles he wrote near the end of the last century.

Here's a condensation:

1. Hard work is good for you.
2. Thrift is good for you.
3. Make good investments.
4. Good investments will make you rich.
5. Rich is good for you—and the country.
6. Giving it away is good for you.
7. Having it left when you die is bad.
8. Even worse—it's a disgrace for you.

There's the gospel. Carnegie believed it. Such luck for everyone. At least for everyone who likes reading and listening to organ music, striving for peace or being a hero.

Carnegie Public Library grew out of an experience during his teens in Pittsburgh. A generous person had granted access to a library free to indentured youths, but charged a $2 fee to all others. Carnegie was not indentured, wanted books, and $2 represented a week's wage. He went to battle writing letters to the Pittsburgh Dispatch. He won. The $2 charge was dropped. FREE PUBLIC LIBRARY was now engraved in his mind. Carnegie's tussle to obtain free books for himself would, in time, translate to free books for most of America, from the Atlantic to the Pacific, from the Great Lakes to the Gulf. This great philanthropist is the patron saint of libraries—2500 of them throughout the USA and many more overseas.

His crown jewel was bequeathed to Pittsburgh—"The Carnegie." It focuses on four disciplines: Art, Literature, Science and Music—plus a library, of course. Four seated figures, symbolic "Greats" out of history, welcome you to the marble edifice on Forbes Avenue in Schenley Park. Pause as you enter and imagine you are sharing this experience with Michelangelo, Shakespeare, Galileo and Bach.

Since its inception, many other benefactors have added donations to create a conglomerate of legacies. So much so that the visitor will need at least a day, and more if special events are being featured, to really take in "The Carnegie."

The Carnegie Music Hall (not to be confused with Carnegie Hall in Manhattan) seats over 2,000 and is home to numerous musical groups. Its marble and gilt foyer is one of the world's most elegant. The walls are of French eschallion. Twenty-four pillars of green "vert tinos" stone extend to a splendid gold baroque ceiling. It has the ambiance of the Edwardian Age.

The Hall of Architecture contains the largest collection of plaster casts in America, and replicates many of the great masterpieces of ancient Egypt, Greece, Rome and Renaissance Europe. They are placed in chronological order to help you with your history. The dimensions of the hall are based on the Mausoleum of Halicarnassus, one of the seven wonders of the ancient world.

The Hall of Sculpture is crafted of the finest Pentaelic marble, taken from the same quarries in Greece which supplied marble to build the Parthenon.

Carnegie urged that The Museum of Art collect the "Old Masters of Tomorrow." There are paintings by Monet, Matisse, Bonnard, Degas, also Homer and Whistler. (Carnegie wanted all nudes draped . . .)

The Museum of Natural History ranges in scope from planetary faults to the polar world. There's also the "Home of the Dinosaurs," an impressive assemblage of bones to teach us something about why not to become extinct.

On a wall in these corridors you may note a message in marble. It was penned by the colonial leader destined to become the second president of the United States. One hundred years later, Andrew Carnegie was echoing the same resolve.

I must study politics and war that my sons may have liberty to study mathematics and philosophy. My sons are to study mathematics and philosophy . . . in order to give their children a right to study painting, poetry, music, and architecture.

John Adams
in a letter to wife Abigail
May 12, 1780

There are other reasons to visit Pittsburgh. As American journalist Brandon Gill wrote, "If Pittsburgh were situated somewhere in the heart of Europe, tourists would eagerly journey hundreds of miles out of their way to visit it."

Heinz Hall: The structure evolved, from its origin in 1927 as the Penn Theater to renovation and dedication as Heinz Hall for the Performing Arts in 1971. It is "a gift to the Pittsburgh Symphony Society from the Howard Heinz Endowment . . . to encourage, foster and perpetuate the performing arts in the Greater Pittsburgh area." Built as a plush movie house by motion picture magnate Marcus Loew, the old Penn Theater featured excellent acoustics and a plush decor of cream with green draperies, black and white marble pillars and large crystal chandeliers.

In 1974 the theater closed its doors and stood vacant. The city was considering tearing it down and replacing it with a parking lot when the Pittsburgh Symphony Society approached the Heinz Foundation. A special pops concert under the direction of Doc Severinson proved that the building was still usable. With a burst of creative energy; together with the support of the Heinz foundation, corporate giants, and numerous individual contributors, a $10-million reconstruction was completed.

Much of the basic architecture of the building remains unchanged from the original French court style. The 40-foot Hunt window, which was donated by Alcoa, replaced the original entrance and rises above the Grand Lobby. Two 15-foot chandeliers weighing more than a ton each, are spectacular attractions in the Grand Lobby.

The 1986-87 season was the occasion for a triple anniversary in Heinz Hall: the 90th Anniversary of the founding of the Pittsburgh Symphony, the 60th Anniversary of the Pittsburgh Symphony Society and the 15th Anniversary year for Heinz Hall. It was a well-deserved tribute to the late Henry J. Heinz II, whose vision and leadership largely created Pittsburgh's Cultural District.

Pittsburgh is awash in legacies. The money fallout here is too vast to cover in the space available. Names like Mellon, Phipps, Frick, and a score of Carnegie's entourage, have all left this city well endowed. Pittsburgh merits several days which leads to where to stay. The Westin William Penn Hotel is a classic. Belongs to the history of the region, and to the city's Renaissance II, a $2.4-billion rebirth program started in the 70s.

The building of the William Penn Hotel was one of the last ventures of Henry Clay Frick, an early Carnegie associate and donor of New York City's Frick Museum of Art. This magnificent hotel opened in 1916 with Mr. Frick in the presidential suite. It was designed by Pittsburgh's architectural firm, Janssen and Abbott. They created a three-towered, 900-bedroom masterpiece of a hotel which provided the ultimate luxury for its guests. A bathroom for every room! Electric lights, so no candles need be used! Recent reno-restorations to the tune of $30 million have moved the William Penn into the jet-set age in step with the Golden Triangle.

A lot of memories are locked in these great dining and dancing halls. Many a big-name band has beamed across the nation from the William Penn, including Lawrence Welk. "Champagne Music" was born here and over the years there have been lots of "bubbles in the wine."

National Architect magazine, extolling the William Penn after completion, thought this a noteworthy comment: "A unique feature of the hotel is that the 15th floor has been set aside solely for the use of bachelors." Well! The country sees things differently nowadays, so see you in court on that one.

Social change doesn't stop with unisexing the 15th floor. On the concourse level Rotary meets on Tuesday. I didn't attend, but I'm willing to bet that ladies are welcome there, too.

Seiberling Home, Akron, Ohio,
Courtesy of Stan Hywet Hall Foundation, Inc.

Stan Hywet Hall

A creative couple, solidly married, developed and then gave to Akron a substantial country manor. For obscure reasons, they preferred that it carry a name meaning "stonehewn"—which it is. The stones came from a quarry on the property.

Stan Hywet Hall is the home built by F.A. and Gertrude Seiberling for their family. It provided warmth and camaraderie for seven children, many guests, relatives and events. It set an occupancy record for mansions, as it was home to one family for more than forty years. Edgar Guest described Stan Hywet when he penned "it takes a heap of living to make a house a home!"

F.A. Seiberling and his brother, Charles, founded the Goodyear Tire and Rubber Company. He was one of this nation's industrial leaders and helped make Akron the rubber capital to the emerging automobile age. The money from rubber allowed F.A. to create a most impressive dwelling place, which now belongs to the public.

Stan Hywet was designed by a noted Cleveland architect, Charles S. Schneider. Initially it was surrounded by 3,000 acres. Warren Manning did the landscape design for the formal seventy acres, which includes a lagoon, a waterfall and sundry delights which are still part of the estate.

Visitors will find Stan Hywet easier to comprehend than the other extravaganzas described in this book. It has "livability—believability" on a grand scale, including a great hall, Chinese room, music room, fountain room, billiard room, and half-a-hundred more. The wood carvings alone took three years for expert craftsmen to complete.

The music room was the favorite of Mrs. Seiberling. Dozens of famous musicians performed here: Paderewski, Fritz Kreisler, Rosa Ponselle, Madame Schumann Heink and Leopold Stokowski, among others.

Gertrude Penfield Seiberling—wife, mother, hostess and gracious lady—was also an artist, musician and connoisseur of collectables. She and her husband traveled extensively in Europe, making choices and searching tirelessly for accessories to complete their Akron home. Most remains as it was when used by the family.

Seiberling's giant ideas allowed him to stand tall among Akron's rubber barons. He lost his Goodyear Rubber Company, but rose again with another tire company which bore his name, and made another fortune. His accomplishments might suggest a giant ego, but all we know about F.A. indicates that he was a humble, generous man with many friends. Characteristically, the Seiberlings intended that Stan Hywet Hall eventually be their legacy to the public. This "greeting" by Gertrude Seiberling says it convincingly:

Greetings

On heights o'erlooking rolling woodland
And distant valley's purple shadows . . .
Stan Hywet rests, and sends you greeting . . .
The truth is old that walls and roof tree
However fine ne'er make a home . . .
So as the months and years unfold
Joy will they bring as joy we need
If you kind friends but enter in . . .
And make our house a home indeed.

"Okay, we've seen Stan Hywet Hall. Very impressive," you say. "But now that we're in Akron for the night, what do we do?" True, Akron is not the hub of much. Once, all of our tires came from Akron; that's over. The city was also Rex Humbard's TV-evangelism launch pad; he's gone (moved closer to the Bible Belt). It's the highest point in Ohio and home to a pro-football Hall of Fame. But let's not panic. You like trains, don't you? Well, how about a unique hotel with some racy railroad action? You won't believe this hotel, though, unless you believe in oatmeal.

Some people think the "winning of the West" was a testimonial for the Winchester 30-30 rifle. Not so. Oatmeal did it. Same holds true for the Civil War. It's said that an army moves on its stomach. Civil War stomachs were full of oatmeal. Lots of companies once milled oats. But Quaker became the household word for breakfast oats. Since nobody this side of the Atlantic knew how good it was, some promotion was needed. Quaker knew how to get a housewife's attention. They slid a dish into every package. In time, the whole country was eating from Quaker Oats dishes.

In our house you knew the weather was bad if the Quaker Oats box was out on the counter top. Mothers just knew hot oatmeal was necessary to get the kids to school through a blizzard—it's stored-up heat would ward off frostbite. And mothers always cooked more than needed. That gave the cat and the dog, the pigs and the chickens a lift, too.

This country was once an industrial dynamo. Exported our surplus. Then junk food supplanted oatmeal for breakfast. We've been on the skids ever since.

Today's news says our children graduating from school are illiterate. This must have all started with kids being sent to school on junk food breakfasts. There once was a time kids walked to school no matter what the weather—they were steamed up on oatmeal. Nowadays a diet Pepsi-Coke only gets them to the bus. And school gets cancelled for icy streets, strikes, shootings and flooded intersections.

Quaker Oats came in a round box with a taped-on top. There was a pull-string to break the tape, but it never did and the top got freed with a knife. But carefully, because the box was nearly as important as the contents. The round oatmeal box never was trashed. Too valuable. It was used in the sewing room to hold yarn and patches; needed in the tool shed for nuts and bolts and nails. Great for cookies under the Christmas tree. Biodegradable too: generally wound up starting the fire in the kitchen range. Always recycled.

The mill from which oatmeal came has been recycled too. The

Quaker Oats Company moved out of Akron, leaving all these round storage silos with eight-inch concrete walls. They looked like a white elephant—to everyone but a CPA named Jay Nusbaum. He thought they looked like a hotel. Crazy?

The Quaker Oats Hotel is not run-of-the-mill. Ever sleep in a silo? You can here. It's an ingenious conversion job with balconies for each room and many other amenities.

Every grain elevator hangs out alongside the railroad. The "Silo-Hilton" turned its siding into an entertainment mecca. There is a big train, but—better yet—there are model trains. And where did model trains come from? In 1900, a 20-year-old inventor concealed a small electric motor and a battery under a simple wooden flat car and sent it traveling around a small circle of brass track. It didn't look like much, by modern standards, but it was new and unique and it ran under its own power, a feat never before achieved. Joshua Lionel Cowen had conceived an idea that, as it grew, brought delight to millions of children, young and old, and became an American tradition.

Go through the Quaker Oats Hotel lobby, out to the depot. Push a button and model trains race in all directions. Dozens of them. They whistle, they whiz through town; they bring the circus, they clickety-clack over bridges. Whee-e-e!

Tonight you can sleep in a silo alongside the tracks and dream about trains and rural America and you're only 1500 miles east of free ice-water at Hustead's Drug Store in Wall, South Dakota!

I SLEPT
IN A SILO!

QUAKER SQUARE HILTON

★ ★ ★ Mobil ◆ ◆ ◆ ◆ 🅰🅰🅰

DOWNTOWN ● AKRON, OHIO

*Listed in The National Register
of Historic Places*

GUIDE TO GREENFIELD VILLAGE

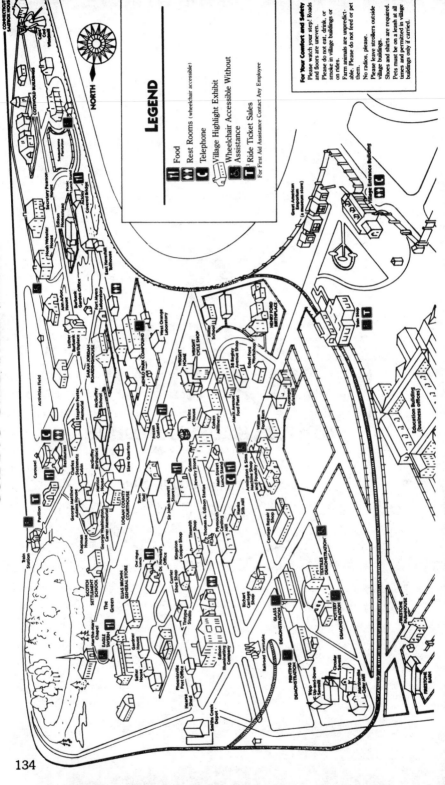

LEGEND

🍴 Food

🚻 Rest Rooms (wheelchair accessible)

📞 Telephone

Village Highlight Exhibit

♿ Wheelchair Accessible Without Assistance

T Ride Ticket Sales
For First Aid Assistance Contact Any Employee

For Your Comfort and Safety
Please watch your step! Roads and floors are uneven.
Please do not eat, drink, or smoke in village buildings or on rides.
Farm animals are unpredictable. Please do not feed or pet them.
No radios, please.
Please leave strollers outside village buildings.
Shoes and shirts are required.
Pets must be on a leash at all times and permitted in village buildings only if carried.

NORTH

Greenfield Village
Henry Ford

"It will take a hundred years to tell whether he helped us or hurt us, but he certainly didn't leave us where he found us."

—Will Rogers

Henry Ford Museum/Greenfield Village is about inventions; about geniuses as well as ordinary men and women who, with common sense and hard work, built America.

Here, among steam-powered cars, Franklin stoves and hand-cranked washing machines, you'll discover how imaginative minds transformed our nation. In historic homes, vintage workshops and a working 19th-century farm, you'll come to know how our ancestors lived.

At Henry Ford Museum, under 80 acres of roof, you'll see fascinating examples of the unusual stuff that entertained and sustained America. Threshing machines and pioneer aircraft. Silver, glass, furniture and jewelry. Farm machinery that depended on real-life horses—and carriages that didn't. Cars with names like Stanley Steamer, Stutz and Studebaker; elegant classics and fondly-remembered family sedans. There is a genuine 1946 Massachusetts roadside diner. A 1950s drive-in theater with movies still running. A Holiday Inn guest room from the 1960s.

In Greenfield Village, take a walk or carriage ride to houses and shops where famous Americans lived and worked. See the Menlo Park laboratory where Edison invented so brilliantly; the Connecticut home where Noah Webster wrote his famous dictionary; the Dayton bicycle shop where the Wright Brothers' dreams first took flight.

Visit machine shops, sawmills, forges and other workplaces, and gain a keener sense of the dynamic spirit that transformed this country into a modern power. Watch village artisans and workers ply their olden trades. Around every corner you'll come face-to-face with America's past.

The Museum/Village is Ford's salute to that era of American history when the door flung wide open to mechanical inventors. When 19th Century lifestyle was screaming for labor-saving contraptions. Henry Ford was there with his Model T.

Search out the Model T. When you find it, embrace it. For you are then joined with Henry Ford's pet, and you are in the presence of a primitive contraption that transformed a culture.

Model T? Have you ever wondered whatever happened to "A" through "S"? Imagine a time when there were no computers, no copy machines, and no graduating class of mechanical engineers to recruit. Without schooling and without precedent, here comes Ford, a madcap tinkerer with the crazy obsession that he can improve on the horse and buggy. One idea built on another, and after years of moonlighting and innovating and using up the alphabet with model after model—the "T" was ready for the ruts and bumps and mudholes. Experimentation had evolved a design worthy of production: "T"—for "Tin Lizzie." Henry's goal was a Ford in every driveway: "I'm going to democratize the automobile. When I'm through everybody will be able to afford one and about everyone will have one . . . The automobile will be taken for granted and there won't be any problem." Not many people believed Henry Ford when he spoke these words. Eighty years later, this prophecy is a good one to think about as you choke on smog while inching along the freeway. Ford was not alone. There were a hundred better-qualified inventors moving in the same direction. Most of them went broke. Only a few saw their names on the hood/bonnet. None became a legend—except Crazy Henry.

It was a new century, launched with wheels. The Ford became the common folk's car (in an era when there were a lot of such people). Henry's "Tin Lizzie" gave mobility to the farm and to the tenement. He made a mechanic of everyone who had a pair of pliers and a strand of baling wire, and put the driver's life in danger of a lethal weapon called a hand crank! It hung below the vehicle and, when the engine backfired, could tear out a shoulder ligament. I speak from experience! In time, Ford's good friend, Thomas Edison, replaced the crank with an electric starter, and eliminated much profanity.

Once his unimposing assemblage of iron and isinglass was assured success, Ford built an industrial cathedral to produce it. The Highland Park plant introduced the assembly line, and was hailed as the marvel of production and the curse of machine-induced boredom. When Ford made a bold leap to the $5 wage—per day, that is—his adoring public was so enthralled by a living wage, and so relieved to find affordable wheels to ease their poor aching feet, they lofted him into folklore. "Ford for President!" became an oft-heard acclamation.

He was the only one to do battle with the "Selden Patent", a monopolistic claim to the internal-combustion engine. The rest of the industry caved in, but not Ford, even though he lost the first round. Also lost his cause with a peace ship to stop the war (WWI). Lost his run for the senate (ran "independent" of course and lost, but not by much). Lost, or gave up, his anti-semitism crusade. Lost and/or ran off one key associate after another. For an habitual loser, he sure ended up rich.

Unlike the rich, Ford was a stubborn, simple and modest next-door neighbor, diligently puttering in his workshop. He puttered with such success that he acquired more money than any industrialist of that era—a sum so vast he had little choice but to create a foundation. It was odd, whatever the tax-induced reason, for him to surrender control of anything, especially his wealth. Thereafter, the Ford Foundation conveyed money to debatable recipients, most of whom old Henry would have denounced. This is only one of the many baffling riddles about this scion of the auto age.

Ford was the work ethic spokesman: "I do not believe in charity, but I do believe in the regenerating power of work in men's lives." He frequently mistook frustration for inspiration and got into more crusades than made sense. He started the auto age as the driving force and ended as a restraining force. In time, General Motors rolled over him and so did the calendar. Like his Model T, Henry Ford succumbed to obsolescence—but not before he left one giant footprint on the pages of history.

He launched his museum in 1929 and named it The Edison Institute. Here Henry Ford could retreat into an era that he could manage and understand.

His museums are a stroll through time. The Appendix gives directions to locate them. One or two days invested there will bridge several generation gaps. And you'll discover why your grandparents didn't have a problem with spare time before television.

> *"History is bunk," Ford said. "I'm going to start up a museum and give people a true picture of the development of our country. That's the only history that is worth preserving. We're going to build a museum that's going to show industrial history, and it won't be bunk."*
>
> from reminiscences of Ernest Liebold

Photo courtesy of Jefferson National Expansion Memorial, NPS

The Arch
Grant's Farm /
Missouri Botanical Garden

10:00 a.m., October 28, 1965: The moment of truth. A vast gathering of the St. Louis faithful and skeptics were gazing skyward to witness an engineering triumph—or the boo-boo of the century. Consider: two triangular spindles, heaven-bound monsters supported only by a root sixty feet down into the sub-strata with bases 630 feet apart. Now these towering stems, taller than a 60-story skyscraper, were reaching to be joined.

One thousand days earlier, their bottom sections had been planted on massive concrete foundations. These equilateral triangles of stainless steel had, at ground level, measured fifty-four feet along each side. One hundred and seventy-one sections upward, they tapered to seventeen feet. Now the last one, an eight-foot capstone, would close the gap—hopefully.

From the start it was known the positioning of the two bases must be precise; the points of the triangle must align perfectly; the twelve-foot sections in each leg must be identical twins and not even 1/16-of-an-inch deviation was acceptable. One undetected error in measurement could spell disaster.

Now, after years of daytime hoisting and nighttime measuring, the two legs were ready to be joined by that final section. At that moment, watched by thousands along the muddy Mississippi, the missing link slowly rose on its cable . . . . Will it fit? The foreman on top was connected by phone to the engineer on the ground:

"Hey BOSS! It looks like the south leg is eleven inches high . . . . "

Chief Engineer: "The damn sun is doing it. We have the fire department hosing down from 500 feet to cool it."

"Boss, there's more. How we supposed to jam eight feet into a thirty-inch slot? You tell me . . . . "

Chief: "Use the hydraulic force to spread the legs. That's why you've got 400 tons of push."

"Boss, we're at 320 tons, it still won't fit, and the men are ready to jam this job."

Chief: "Grease it in—that's what I'm paying you for, damn it!"

True story? No, it's what might have been. When that last section of the St. Louis Arch slid into place about noontime that fall day in 1965, the engineers had sunk a 630-foot putt. On the ground below, the crowd held its breath. People staring skyward fidgeted and prayed.

It worked. It fit. Two great twins at last embraced—no longer in a limitless sky. They were an ARCH. At last.

From that moment, this great towering monument began a thousand-year testimony to industrial engineering, to the skills of man, to Jefferson, to the pioneers of the West and to the persevering people of St. Louis. It is a celebration of the past and a pledge to the future! [1]

"Go west young man"—through the Gateway Arch. Horace Greeley? Yes; echoing a much earlier visionary: Thomas Jefferson, a foresighted president who grasped the importance of the mighty Mississippi and the land beyond. He commissioned Lewis and Clark

---

[1] A sad footnote: missing from the crowd watching the capstone suspense was one whose name is part of the monument—Eero Saarinen. He had predicted his design would endure for a millenium. The grim reaper was not so charitable toward the creator. His widow was his surrogate witness of the event.

to explore the immensity of the West, and pioneers who followed demonstrated its value. The Arch memorializes them.

One hundred and sixty years after the Louisiana Purchase, St. Louis paid tribute to an epic slice of U.S. history. This monumental rainbow of glistening steel speaks of foresight—courage—determination—productivity—growth! The Arch was born out of the same stubbornness that opened the West, that plowed the prairies, that endured the hazards of the trail.

No sodbuster's future was any bleaker than the prospect that this arch could really happen. How did it come about? Why along the bank of "ol' man river"?

It seems that a public-spirited person named Smith was riding by rail into St. Louis across the now-revered Eads Bridge. A companion was giving him a lesson in history:

"Why, that blighted riverbank is filled with more history per square mile than any piece of property west of the great river. It is a disgrace to let such hallowed ground become so neglected . . . . "

This seed lodged in the mind of Luther Ely Smith, haunted him, and set him on a course that consumed his remaining years. It was dream time and the year was 1933. Initially, Mr. Smith envisioned only a river-front park. But ideas grow. This one grew into a committee which went into action, and by 1934, presto—the Jefferson National Expansion Memorial Association (JNEMA), its working name, "Jenny May." With Mr. Smith as its chairman, Jenny May had commitment; it had heart. What it didn't have was money.

Federal aid seemed the most likely source. But not an easy one—a lesson that Gutzon Borglum was learning with much pain, a few hundred miles upstream where Mount Rushmore languished for funds. Federal money might not be forthcoming, but a blessing was. President Roosevelt made it official in 1934 and again in 1935 with an executive order declaring there would indeed be a monument to Jefferson, to his aides (Livingston and Monroe), to the Louisiana Purchase, and to Lewis and Clark. Just around the corner it was—a corner that would take thirty years to turn.

Initially, about all that was known of the memorial's substance was that the "Old Courthouse" would be included. This Greek Revival antiquity dates back to 1839, has a dome with murals, a lot of sentiment and some dubious fame as the trial location for the Dred Scott Decision. (That was a landmark legal labyrinth that wound through numerous courts over thirteen years and helped nudge the country into the Civil War.)

By 1947 enough obstacles had been surmounted to sponsor a competition. There were 172 submissions and the first prize of $50,000 went to Eero Saarinen, a Finnish-American architect. Saarinen's concept was a catenary arch, a design that allows the thrust to pass through to the foundations (thank goodness!)—630 feet high, 630 feet separating the two bases. The bases were to be joined underground, with an area to house a museum, reception area and a transporter to lift visitors to the top.

An ARCH! Tapering triangle form. Tough to design and tougher to construct. But to those in command it probably seemed a pushover compared to thirteen years of weaving through a mine field of politics and finance. Luckily the supporters could not foresee another fifteen years of overcoming obstacles before ground breaking.

Construction was stressful, chilling, and no place for an acrophobic. Luckily a movie was made, so visitors can view the process. For thirty white-knuckle minutes you can dangle with workmen high above the streets. Even in the comfort of the theater I was rigid. And when that last section slid into place, I shared the thrill—and was ready to scurry down to the ground.

Paul Simpson McElroy has an eloquent summary of the Gateway Arch:

"Man needs today, as in every age, to attempt something that will challenge his ingenuity and resources to the maximum. It matters not whether the project be a magnificent temple or a tremendous tomb, a pretentious palace or a fabulous plaza, the significant thing is that such undertakings be of sufficient magnitude to challenge the resourcefulness and the abilities of the entire nation, and this Saarinen Arch soaring gracefully and grandly over the riverfront has captured the imaginations of people all over the world. It may not be classified as one of the seven wonders of the modern world, but it has required all the ingenuity of modern engineering and it is the dominating feature of the city."

from *The Story of the Gateway Arch*
by Paul Simpson McElroy

Museum of Westward Expansion

A century of American History in the underground Visitors' Center has a unique way of making the subject tasty. For an inquiring mind, a day here should be worth a month of classroom history or geography. You are in a National Park facility, and the rangers are here to guide you on your westward migration.

Do you love Western movies when the Indians attack the wagon trains and shoot flaming arrows to ignite wagon covers? "Pure Hollywood," the ranger tells us. The Indians were too smart for that. They

145

didn't want the smelly oxen (too slow) nor the creaky wagons (too clumsy) nor the bleached-out maidens (too skinny). Those canvas wagon covers were the prize they wanted. Instant tents, bed covers, ponchos.

Here in this museum you learn from the ranger that the prairie sodbusters were our original land bargain hunters. For a buck-and-a-quarter an acre, the settler could buy from Uncle Sam the right to sweat out a chunk of the good earth. And since the Louisiana Purchase cost Jefferson's government a mere four cents an acre, the U.S. turned a tidy profit.

A thought-provoking article by James R. Chiles (Smithsonian, March 1984) compares the possible life expectancy of this arch with that of the ancient wonders of the world. It speculates that if all maintenance should cease (most unlikely) and luck spares it of earthquakes and tornadoes, the Arch should endure for hundreds of years. The lower 300 feet, which is substantially concrete, might last another 5,000 years. Let us not fret. 'Ere that expiration date, this towering landmark will have signalled its welcome to a lot of traffic up and down the mighty Mississippi.

Grant's Farm

This 280-acre estate of August A. Busch, Jr., is open to the public and tours are free. It salutes the Civil War commander and 18th President of the U.S. (Grant) who once lived here and farmed part of the grounds. It is not easy to visit unless you have your own auto. The Appendix gives some help.

Gussie Busch was a St. Louis patriarch, a beer-baron out of the past who had a love affair with St. Louis. His company was first in the beer industry and his baseball team, the Cardinals, won their share of baseball pennants. Busch was a tough, bombastic, civic leader of the sort they just don't make anymore. He was also a philanthropist, and Grant's Farm is part of his legacy. His ninth inning ended September 29, 1989, when he retired to the dug-out for keeps.

The Missouri Botanical Gardens

This garden is a seventy-nine-acre attraction worthy of half a day, even if you're not into growing things. It is our legacy from Henry Shaw, an early St. Louis merchant. Born at Sheffield, England in the year 1800, he left at age eighteen to seek his fortune. Apparently he took with him a typical British love of botany. Shaw found his business opportunity in St. Louis, began importing cutlery from his native Sheffield, then speculated in land and made a fortune sufficient to load his vast acreage with garden specimens from all over the world including many fountains and thirty or so prize sculptures—one of which, the last, he commissioned for his own tomb. A marble effigy awaiting the final date—1889. It is now part of the tour.

NOTES:

1. In a sequel to follow this book, the focus will expand to great edifices inspired by religious energy. It will include the St. Louis Cathedral, a 1907 Byzantine, Romanesque miracle-in-mosaic from vault to dome. The Appendix tells how to locate it . . . and you must.

2. The attractions in this book have been sequenced geographically to fit a driving itinerary, sort of. Two exciting subjects which will be covered in the sequel are a routing dog-leg to or from St. Louis. The House on the Rock (Spring Green) and the Circus Museum (Baraboo) are in the Madison, Wisconsin area. (See Chapter 5.) They are out of the way but worth the effort.

23

Mount Rushmore

"A Cornerstone Laid by the Hand of the Almighty"
—President Calvin Coolidge (1927 dedication)

Mount Borglum! That's what it should be renamed. I have nothing against Charles Rushmore as a person. He was, possibly, a good mining lawyer. That role accounts for his climbing around the Black Hills early in this century. But it is a disservice to the most awesome sculpture on this planet for its pedestal not to proclaim the name of the artist.

The four granite countenances that dominate the mountainscape in these Black Hills are bigger than politics, and the sculptor who made it happen was in their league. The foolish suggestion occasionally sneaks into the news that someone's favorite president should be added. A fifth! It would be sacrilege to touch this creation. But were it to happen, the only fitting face to add would be that of Gutzon Borglum.

Borglum chose four presidents to occupy this 5725-foot-high granite dais. From this lofty command post they look out across the vast country they loved. Borglum rarely minced words:

> "If America wants a product of art; if America wants an interpretation of Washington's character, of Jefferson's intelligence, of Lincoln's vision and soul, of Theodore Roosevelt's force and modernness—then she must trust to the judgment, insight and understanding of an artist."

Only a crazy man would have attempted such a gigantic carving. Only a congenital optimist would have believed the financing could be raised. Only a dedicated dreamer would have toughed it out for fourteen years. Only a genius would bring it to within a cosmetic touch of completion.

Other key figures were crucial to its creation, of course. Doane Robinson, State Historian, who first had the vision; U.S. Senator Peter Norbeck, who worked to keep the appropriations rolling; John Boland, Congressman William Williamson and others tried to maintain order and control a cantankerous artist—not always successfully. Borglum was a runaway, the others tried to steer.

The President of the United States christened this project, August 10, 1927, with the words:

" . . . On this towering wall of Rushmore, in the heart of the Black Hills, is to be inscribed a memorial which will represent some of the outstanding events of American history . . . laid on by the hand of a great artist in sculpture . . . . "

For "Silent Cal" that was a mouthful. Succeeding presidents Hoover and Roosevelt added vital support. But only Coolidge could utter such an underwhelming tribute.

Gutzon Borglum was not noted for humility, but there was a bit of humble philosophy in a statement he gave to the Black Hill Engineer, printed in its November 1930 bulletin: "There is something here that is related to God in His Heaven, aeons older than the pinhead sculptor, something that relates itself and ourselves to a universe of gods which super-civilization, as I see it, seems ever to be reaching towards."

Gutzon was old when he started, nearing sixty, but he neither knew it nor felt it. Ahead lay fourteen years of frustration dealing with political orneriness, financial obstacles and delays waiting for money. On numerous occasions he bolstered the bank account with his own funds (not easy for a person who was often overdrawn). He misread big supporters and sometimes felt betrayed, misunderstood and plagued by enemies, real and imagined. Often times involved with lost causes, his monument remained always his holy grail.

That Borglum missed seeing his monument completed is somewhat consistent with his life. He left a string of failed missions, but who's to say it was tragic? Maybe it was his destiny. What is certain is that those majestic faces on that magnificent mountain will endure for the ages. A thousand winters will not dim those piercing expressions. Mount Rushmore is forever!

Borglum died March 6, 1941, at age seventy-four. Earlier he had voiced a wish to finish his days in California. He got his wish posthumously. He is buried at Forest Lawn Cemetery in Glendale.

Luckily for us, the viewing public, John Gutzon de la Mothe Borglum had a son who shared his father's passion. Lincoln Borglum was a key player in the completion of the monument. He had talent and had worked closely enough with the sculptor to take over the project in his father's waning years, and to finish it some eight months after his father's death.

Your visit to this heritage will be enriched if you read in advance Lincoln Borglum's *MOUNT RUSHMORE, The Story Behind the Scenery* (KC Publications).

Lincoln Borglum is also deceased now. He left this powerful statement to attest to his high regard for his father:

> "As a national memorial Rushmore is unique. Pictures of Mount Rushmore are almost univerally recognized. It is a satisfaction to know that long after the death of its sculptor—long after generations of his descendants have come and gone—there in the center of the continent his monument will stand, an astonishing, enduring record of the history of the United States and an eloquent testament to his love for his country."

There is no time more fitting to experience this place than the evening of the Fourth of July. Join in the national Park Service rally at the amphitheater. Watch the flag wave, sing the Star Spangled Banner, admire the flood-lit faces on the mountain. One leaves the mountain proud of our national heritage. I know, because such was my good fortune.

151

"I want, somewhere in America on or near the Rockies, the backbone of the Continent, so far removed from succeeding, selfish, coveting civilizations, a few feet of stone that bears witness, carries the likenesses, the dates, aword or two of the great things we accomplished as a Nation, placed so high it won't pay to pull down for lesser purposes.

Hence, let us place there, carved high, as close to heaven as we can, the words of our leaders, their faces, to show posterity what manner of men they were. Then breathe a prayer that these records will endure until the wind and the rain alone shall wear them away."

Gutzon Borglum

The Sculptor's Story at Keystone

If the faces on Mount Rushmore were completed, same scale, to full body dimensions; were it possible to stand Lincoln alongside the Statue of Liberty, her uplifted torch would only reach his belt. A full-bodied Jefferson could wade the Mississippi to visit his St. Louis Memorial and not get his knees wet. That's standing tall!

Their sculptor also stood mighty tall. To fully appreciate Gutzon Borglum, visit the "RUSHMORE-BORGLUM STORY." His life and works are on display at the roadside settlement of Keystone, enroute from Rapid City to the Memorial. There is a short film to let you feel the fear and challenge of dangling on the mountain's sheer walls with Borglum, plus witnessing the individual dedications as each face was completed. You can have a self-guided-carry-your-own-sound-track event. It is an eye-opener.

This "Borglum Memorial" is the creation of Dr. Duane Pankratz. Howard and Audrey Shaff have been key contributors and are the current directors. Their book *Six Wars at a Time* is an exciting account of Borglum's amazing antics. There's a modest admission charge; it is less than the cost of parking your car for a big-city attraction.

This interlude will make your Rushmore experience a one-hundred per center.

High Hopes - Crazy Horse!

When the legends die, the dreams end;
When the dreams end, there is no more greatness

Korczak

One of Borglum's assistants, a promising and talented Polish sculptor with determination, must have caught mountain fever from Gutzon, because he embarked on an even more ambitious mission at the invitation of Sioux Chief, Henry Standing Bear.

Korczak Ziolkowski found a higher mountain, seventeen miles southwest of Rushmore, and agreed to sculpt it.

This wild artist bought the hunk of granite with his own funds (he had precious little). Without government help—or interference—he started a project he knew he would not live to see finished: Crazy Horse—a Sioux Warrior who distinguished himself during the Indian wars of the 1800s.

A lot of mysticism underlies the project. By coincidence, Korczak was born on the day Crazy Horse was stabbed to death by a white soldier thirty-one years earlier—Sept. 6, 1877. During his lifetime, Crazy Horse told his people he would return to them in stone, and he often wore a protective stone talisman at his ear. He died in his early thirties.

Crazy Horse is being recreated as a memorial to his spirit and to his people. The carving has his left hand thrust ahead, pointing as if in answer to the derisive question once asked by a white man: "Where are your lands now?" His reply: "My lands are where my dead lie buried."

By some irony, the shape of Thunderhead Mountain dictated that Crazy Horse's outthrust arm point toward the town of Custer, named for the nemesis of Native American injustice.

Korczak Ziolkowski was a huge man with an indomitable spirit.

Crazy Horse Memorial

HEIGHT:

SPHINX	70	ft.
STONE MOUNTAIN (Georgia)	90	ft.
MT. RUSHMORE	285	ft.
President's Heads	60	ft.
PYRAMID OF GIZEH	481	ft.
WASHINGTON MONUMENT	555	ft.
CRAZY HORSE	563	ft.
Indian's Head	90	ft.
Horse's Head	219	ft.

And he had nine lives, judging from the injuries he sustained in pursuing his quest. But nine weren't enough. He died unexpectedly on October 20, 1982, at the age of seventy-four, after thirty years of wrestling with Thunderhead Mountain.

His wife and family, imbued with Korczak's zeal, carried on the work. He left the detailed plans for completion with Ruth Ziolkowski, who is supervising the ongoing activities.

Few of those who read this book will live to see the memorial finished. But it is enough to see the model at the visitor's center about a mile from the carving-in-progress . . . or to make contact with the dedication that permeates this monument. It is worth the drive to tell your grandkids you felt the Spirit.

Theodore Roosevelt said at the Grand Canyon, May 6, 1903:

> "Here is your country. Do not let anyone take it or its glory away from you! Cherish these natural wonders, cherish the History and the Romance as a sacred heritage, for your children and your children's children. DO NOT LET SELFISH MEN OR GREEDY INTERESTS SKIN YOUR COUNTRY of its BEAUTY, its RICHES or its ROMANCE! The world and the Future and your very Children shall judge you according as you deal with this Sacred Trust!"

The Crazy Horse Memorial Foundation welcomes contributions (details of this and the Museum in the Appendix). There is an admission charge, and Lord knows they certainly deserve and need it.

Fairmont Hotel, San Francisco

24

Fairmont Hotel

This famous hotel's story reads like a movie script. We might entitle it: "The Gold Miner's Daughters" (and widows). It has all the crowd-pleasing emotions: rags to riches, love and lust, marriage and divorce, greed and philanthropy. What more does it need to make it an epic? How about earthquake and fire?

As the story begins, Irish kid, James Fair, leaves home in search of a better life and hits the California Gold Rush trail where he teams up with three other young Irish fortune-seekers. Just when life is at its bleakest, the four sons of Ireland strike the greatest single bonanza of precious metal in history. They become the silver kings of Virginia City and split $500 million.

In 1862, Jim Fair marries Theresa Rooney, daughter of the hotel owner in Calaveras County (capital of Mark Twain's frog-jumping contests), and they have two boys (who turn out bad) and two girls (who turn out great). In 1879, Jim buys an election to the U.S. Senate. As Senator Fair he is impotent, but as a womanizer he's front-page copy.

Theresa, however, is a high-class lady who is not about to suffer the indignities of being married to a cad, even if he is a senator. When Mrs. F. divorces Mr. F. (1883), the charge of habitual adultery is worth $5 million. Even at today's scale, $238,095 a year for twenty-one years of marital frustration is pretty fair compensation. The two Fair daughters move with their mother to a fashionable home in San Francisco to be groomed for New York society, while the sons, not the best of boys, stay with the senator.

Here the story heats up. Both the Fair girls catch rich-rich husbands. Tessie marries Herman Oelrichs (heir to Lloyd Lines shipping fortune) and collects a $1 million wedding present from her father. Virginia, lovingly known as Birdie, marries (but not for long) William K. Vanderbilt, II.

Both sisters have tumultuous weddings that strip society's gears. Tessie's is the greatest in San Francisco history, and needs three pages in the newspaper, but Virginia's is the hotter affair. She and William K. spend their wedding night at his parents' Idlehour Mansion on Long Island. The love-nest goes up in flames that very night, and rumor has it that the honeymooners flee to New York City in their sleeping garments—or whatever the beautiful people wear on their wedding night. The loss of one mansion, however, hardly makes a dent in the inventory of great Vanderbilt houses.

The Fair sisters are now entrenched in the fast lane of New York society, which leads to Newport and to partying with their in-laws, the Vanderbilts. To really fit into the society requires a summer cottage (a $50 million mansion needing thirty servants). Tessie and Herman commission Stanford White to design a showplace modeled after the Grand Trianon pleasure-palace of Louis XIV. Rosecliff! It is the most lustrous outcropping of mining money in Newport. Younger sister Virginia isn't left out of the competition because she can lean on her mother-in-law, who has not one, but two Newport summer cottages.

About this time, according to the story line, the two sisters inherit their mother's estate (1891) and then their father's entire estate in 1894—a whopping $45 million, including the choicest view site on Nob Hill in San Francisco. Two years after completing their Newport extravaganza, the Oelrichs focus their attention on this great building site. San Francisco needs a five-star hotel, and the Oelrichs have enough inspiration left over from Rosecliff to make it worthy of the family name: Fairmont.

Two renowned Canadian architects have proven their worth down the coast at the Coronado. Oelrichs commissions them and the project is underway.

The opening of the Fairmont is scheduled for mid-1906. The hotel is nearly finished, and new furnishings are stacked in the lobby in crates. Here the story takes a twist. Enter Herbert and Hartland Law. They fast-talk the sisters Fair into trading the Fairmont for a property-package near the San Francisco waterfront.

It is April 18, 1906. Even the rich-rich are not immune to calamity. The Fair sisters' newly-acquired property is destroyed in the earthquake, only twelve days after the trade, but the Fairmont survives, although with considerable trauma. Fire guts the structure and devours the furnishings . . . a matter of hours after the fire insurance expired.

Now Phoebe Apperson Hearst enters the scene. Another mining-senator's wife-widow with tons of money, she encourages the restoration and completion of the Fairmont. A year to the day after the earthquake, the Fairmont opens. Thereupon, Mrs. Hearst establishes her legal residence in one of its finest suites, and it becomes the command post from which the Pan-Pacific Exposition is planned and financed, as well as the fount from which flows the authority for dispensing inheritances from the Comstock, the Homestake, the Anaconda and a fistful of other mining properties. Then along comes Mrs. Maude Flood, widowed daughter-in-law of one of James Fair's partners. It is 1927. The entire eighth floor became her residence. For the rest of her life, this is home sweet home.[1]

These two custodians of mining fortunes, like two doting grandmothers, lavish art and theater and architecture on a very lucky city. And often the orders pass through the Fairmont doors.

The script played on: Tessie Oelrichs re-acquired the Hotel. Another property trade. This time she swapped forty-six acres of land—land that became the site of the Pan-Pacific Exposition, later becoming known as the Marina District, and later yet, a victim of the 1989 earthquake. The Oelrichs family sold the Fairmont in 1924 to Pasadena hotelman, D.M. Linnard. After World War II, its total capacity was needed to house the United Nations assemblage and the "Flood Penthouse" became headquarters for the U.S. delegation.

---

[1] Although Mrs. Flood claimed that the only way she would leave her Fairmont penthouse was, "feet first, in a box," she generously gave it up temporarily in 1945 for the U.S. delegation to the United Nations convention. It is an immense and opulent suite, the entire eighth floor. As of 1990 it can be rented for $5,000 per night, which may seem a bit stiff but you do get 24-karat, gold-plated bath fixtures and a lot of other extras.

Through its life, the Fairmont has seen several owners and restorations. Now, it has been joined by "Fairmonts" in several other cities, all managed by Richard Swig. The chain recently opened a "Bella Voce," where singing waiters tickle tune-loving ears with musical favorites while serving tasty cuisine. This attraction is a future inducement for this writer, who recalls with fondness drinks at the tower and dinner at Squire's—a best remembrance that has lingered for twenty years.

San Francisco has too many great hotels to cover in this brief account. Across the street from the Fairmont is the Mark Hopkins. It offers a rooftop experience to write home about. Near the old Ferry Terminal is a Hyatt Regency that strains belief. Down Powell Street are several hotels of historic importance, including the St. Francis. This one survived the earthquake of 1906 with some damage. A famous guest barely escaped. Enrico Caruso was there to sing with the Opera Company. He left town in a hurry, got back to New York City, and swore he would never again go near San Francisco; and in fact, would rather sit on Mount Vesuvius.

We salute them all, but believe the Fairmont to be the royal symbol for nesting at San Francisco.

Many movies have been staged at the Fairmont, among them:

Alfred Hitchcock's *Vertigo*.
Kiss Them For Me, starring Cary Grant and Jayne Mansfield.
Petulia, with Julie Christie, George C. Scott and Richard Chamberlain.
Towering Inferno, starring Charlton Heston.
Candice Bergen in *A Night Full of Rain*.
Hagen, with Chad Everett and Arthur Hill.
Carol Burnett and Alan Arkin in *Chu Chu and the Philly Flash*.
Midnight Lace, starring Doris Day.
Diane Keaton and Albert Finney in *Shoot the Moon*.
Sudden Impact, with Clint Eastwood.
Loni Anderson and Lynda Carter in *Partners in Crime* (TV movie).
Lifestyles of the Rich and Famous (TV series).

Map of San Francisco
(Fairmont Hotel is atop Nob Hill, where Powell Street
and California Street Cable Cars intersect.)

SAN FRANCISCO

The exterior of the Beaux Arts Palace camouflages its utilitarian and austere interior. If we need opulence, it is near enough: down the coast at Hearst Castle or back at Nob Hill's regal Fairmont Hotel. Both are legacies funded by mining wealth. By my reckoning, the easier way to strike it rich at Virginia City is to let George Hearst and Jim Fair clamber over the mountains, blister and bruise, sweat and freeze, eat jerky and drink from a canteen, then bring the gold to where we can enjoy it in comfort. I like those old-time prospectors . . . "skookum pardners," as we say in the bush.

25

The Exploratorium

The Golden Gate is your passageway to a golden opportunity--the Exploratorium. This scientific funhouse is a mad scientist's penny arcade—a magic show. Most of all, it is an education. As I told my grandson, "Philip, you can learn more here in a day than in a year of school." He didn't hear me because he was already off to pull levers, peer into boxes, crank wheels.

Excitement vibrates in this cavernous lab. Visitors call to each other, telling friends to "Come see this!"

"Listen to that!"

"Hey, try this!"

Young and old alike hustle between exhibits reading easily-understood explanations and experiencing, by sight or touch or movement, how and why things happen. It's a free-for-all with great purpose.

There are 600 exhibits—antics is a better word—supplemented with visits by specialists, special traveling events, and updates as new knowledge bursts upon us.

This exciting do-it-yourself lab is our legacy from Dr. Frank Oppenheimer. Few scientists' lives can match the drama, controversy and ultimate joy of this noted physicist. Chief among his many contributions to the advancement of science is the Exploratorium, a lasting monument.

Oppenheimer was a victim of the McCarthy era following World War II. Along with his elder brother, J. Robert Oppenheimer, the atom bomb kingpin, Frank lost his job after the war and was forced to give up experimental physics as a result of his brief membership in the Communist Party while a graduate student. Almost overnight, his career changed from brilliant researcher and author to cattle rancher exiled in an isolated region of Colorado, his great talent banished by a phobia that swept the U.S.A.

Born in New York City in 1912, Oppenheimer's early interests were horseback riding, sailing and playing the flute. After only three years, Frank graduated from Johns Hopkins University in 1933 and headed for Europe. He first worked at Rutherford's laboratory in Cambridge. While in England he acquired a pilot's license, then went to the Institute di Arcetri in Florence. A frequent visitor to the Uffizi Gallery, Frank developed a love for art that was rekindled years later in the unlikely setting of the Exploratorium. In the late 1930s, Oppenheimer completed his Ph.D. at the California Institute of Technology, married, then joined the Communist Party out of concern for the plight of the poor. He taught and did research at Stanford University, then joined the Berkeley laboratory of Ernest O. Lawrence, inventor of the cyclotron.

Oppenheimer's work on using electromagnetism to separate uranium isotopes paved the way for his role in helping to build a fission bomb, first at Oak Ridge in Tennessee, then at Los Alamos in New Mexico. In July 1945, with his brother, Frank witnessed Trinity, the first atomic explosion.

Both Oppenheimer brothers had grave concerns about the future in a nuclear world. It was a misgiving shared by many other scientists, and both Oppenheimers spoke out passionately against the bomb. In 1949, Frank was called before the House Un-American Activities Committee. He was forced to resign from the University of Minnesota and give up his research. Oppenheimer's career in experimental physics was at an end.

For ten years, Frank, with his wife and two children, raised cows in the outback. He organized the high school band and taught science in Pagosa Springs, where his students promptly began to win prizes at the state fair. Oppenheimer eventually was invited to re-enter academia at the University of Colorado. Those years as a teacher, Oppenheimer said later, convinced him that the gap between scientists and lay people was becoming dangerously wide. It was a trend he wanted to see reversed.

While on a fellowship at University College, London, Oppenheimer's visit to several European museums influenced his conclusion that America needed a new type of science museum. He believed a museum's virtue lay in teaching about unifying things rather than separating them.

Oppenheimer's experiences as researcher, teacher and impromptu rancher all shaped his conception of the Exploratorium, which opened without fanfare in San Francisco in September 1969. He said: "Explaining science and technology without props is like attempting to tell what it is like to swim without letting a person near the water." He enjoyed recounting the story of the woman who, after visiting the Exploratorium, went home and wired together an electric plug for the first time. She had picked up the Exploratorium's subliminal message that everything in the world is understandable.

The qualities that make the Exploratorium so special are the same that made Dr. Oppenheimer so extraordinary: an insistence upon excellence, a knack for finding new ways of doing things, and a great respect for invention and play. This museum of science, art and human perception now attracts 500,000 visitors a year and has been copied throughout the world. Until his death in 1985 at age seventy-three, Dr. Oppenheimer was still working at the Exploratorium six days a week. Passionately committed to the causes of education, nuclear disarmament and peace, he exemplified a rare combination of two domains—the scientific and the humane.

This exciting mecca for learning occupies most of the Palace of Fine Arts building, located in San Francisco's Marina district near the Golden Gate bridge and adjacent to the Presidio. The structure was designed by renowned architect Bernard Maybeck for the 1915 Panama-Pacific Exposition. Its tenure on earth was meant to be short-lived—all thirty-two of the exposition structures were designed to be savored and scrapped—but the people of San Francisco thought it was too special to perish.

26

The Fine Arts Museums of San Francisco

The two museums that became The Fine Arts Museum of San Francisco were, at one time, rival institutions. A ho-hum observation, you may think—until you learn that the founder of one tried to assassinate the founder of the other. Adolph Spreckels, heir to a sugar fortune, drilled Mike de Young, proprietor of the San Francisco Chronicle, with three bullets. It was a close-range shooting with a .38-calibre revolver—not fatal, though Spreckels was reputed to be a good marksman. The assault occurred on November 19, 1884, at a time when the Wild West still settled its arguments outside the nuisance of the courtroom. It seems that de Young's newspaper printed some unsavory opinions about Spreckel's sugar company, and Adolph couldn't just ignore them. No he-man took an insult lying down. So Adolph did what he had to do . . . shot de Young.

When the judge learned that the victim would live, he released Spreckels without bail, and eventually the case went to trial. Although de Young spent half a year recovering, the jury decided Spreckels wasn't guilty. Maybe the bribes were big enough. Or maybe the jury guessed that, if they were nice to *this* rich-rich man, he'd give the city a museum someday. Which he did.

There's another tie; both museums have roots in an international exposition. The M.H. de Young Memorial Museum grew out of the California midwinter spectacle of 1894. The California Palace of the Legion of Honor, founded by Spreckels and his wife, Alma de Bretteville, had its genesis in the Panama-Pacific Exposition of 1915, the same site the Exploratorium now occupies.

M.H. de Young Memorial Museum

Because 1893 was a year of financial depression in San Francisco, M.H. de Young decided that the West was in need of its own world's fair. As National Commissioner-at-large attending the Columbian Exposition in Chicago in 1893, de Young began to rally public enthusiasm at home—an easy feat since he owned the newspaper. He lobbied until the Golden Gate Park Commission granted some of its land for an exposition, under the condition that the area be returned to the city in such a state that permanent improvements could be carried out on the land. Only five months after the groundbreaking, the California Midwinter International Exposition opened on January 29, 1894, in Golden Gate Park in San Francisco.

Exhibitors at the fair were asked to adhere to exotic Eastern themes, to remind visitors that California, even in January, was another proverbial land of sunshine. In five months, more than 1.3 million enthusiasts visited the buildings erected on the leveled sand dunes of the park. The idea of a permanent museum in Golden Gate Park as an emblem of the exposition was popular, so the fair's executive committee, led by M.H. de Young, offered the Fine Arts building to the park commissioners.

Before long, the museum outgrew its buildings. De Young responded by planning the building that is familiar to de Young Museum visitors today. In 1921, he added a central section, together with the familiar tower, and the museum began to assume its present configuration. That year, his great efforts were honored when his name was given to the museum. Yet another addition, a west wing, was completed in 1925, the year de Young died.

In the 1950s, the de Young Museum received a major gift from the Kress Collection and acquired such masterpieces as *St. Francis Venerating the Crucifix*, by El Greco, and Pieter de Hooch's *Interior with Mother and Children*, as well as choice works by Salomon van Buysdael, Luca di Tomme, Titian and an outstanding work by Giovanni Battista Tiepolo, *The Triumph of Flora*.

The de Young also received a major collection, gift of Mr. and Mrs. Roscoe F. Oakes of San Francisco, that, over a period of years filled five galleries, including an eighteenth-century period room. Among the paintings in the Oakes Collection are Rubens' *Portrait of Rogier Clarisse* and Gabriel Metsu's *Woman Playing a Viola da Gamba*. Hals, Van Dyck, Gainsborough, Reynolds and Raeburn are also represented. In addition, the Oakes' provided a generous fund for art acquisition that continues to enrich the museums.

In the late 1970s, Mr. and Mrs. John D. Rockefeller, III, donated more than one hundred works from their collection of American art, and Mrs. Ednah Root offered to fund a curatorial chair in American art.

Another collection grew impressively when H. McCoy Jones placed his more-than-five-hundred rugs, carpets and embroideries from the Near East and Central Asia in the de Young. The surprise bequest of Teotihuacan murals from the Harald Wagner Estate enriched the collections of art from Africa, Oceania and the Americas. Additionally, the decorative arts collections have benefited from the generosity of Mr. and Mrs. Robert A. Magowan and Mrs. Marriner S. Eccles' support to the European paintings department.

In an attached wing with autonomous governance is the Asian Art Museum. In 1959, Montecito millionaire Avery Brundage offered his vast collection of Asian Art to San Francisco on the condition that the city build a museum to house it. Opened in 1966, the Asian Arts Museum now represents the greatest effort in the Western world to collect, display and study the fine arts of the more than forty countries of Asia. Here, more than 12,000 objects span 6,000 years of history—a legacy from Brundage.

California Palace of the Legion of Honor

In 1915, Alma Spreckels and her husband, the six-shooter sugar magnate, visited the French government's pavilion at the Panama-Pacific Exposition where they viewed an exhibition of sculpture by Auguste Rodin. Mrs. Spreckels had met Rodin the year before. She began her renowned collection of Rodin artifacts with five pieces from the exposition.

The Spreckels were impressed as much by the French pavilion as by its contents. It was a replica of the Palais de la Legion d'Honneur, originally completed in 1788 in Paris as the Hotel de Salm, which Napoleon made the headquarters for his Order of the Legion of Honor. (Another American, Thomas Jefferson, had incorporated the design of its dome into Monticello.) Mrs. Spreckels so admired the building that she offered to construct a permanent replica as an art museum. Considering her husband's gun play with M.H. de Young, however, a site a bit removed from Golden Gate Park seemed preferable.

The focus for the collection of the California Palace of the Legion of Honor was determined at its founding by Alma Spreckels' admiration for French and other European art, although numerous other philanthropists have been major donors.

Archer M. Huntington presented the Legion with a collection of eighteenth-century French paintings, sculpture and tapestries in memory of his father, Collis P. Huntington, a railroad tycoon who launched his nephew into the big money that underwrote the Huntington Library (Chapter 31). H.K.S. Williams and his wife, Mildred Anna Williams, who had no heirs, bequeathed the contents of their house in Paris to the museum and established an endowment.

In 1948, Mr. and Mrs. Moore S. Achenbach created the Foundation for Graphic Arts and presented an entire collection of prints and drawings to the City of San Francisco. Expanded housing for the Achenbach Collection was provided later with a gift from Helene

Irwin Fagan, which added to the museum's collection of medieval art and funded remodeling of the Legion's galleries and offices.

A gift from John D. Spreckels, brother of Adolph, adds melody to the museum. A magnificent organ, built in 1924 by the Skinner Company of Boston, is used for Saturday and Sunday afternoon concerts.

Alma Spreckels placed her own growing collection of Rodin sculptures in the museum. The collection eventually added more than seventy pieces, many of the forty bronzes having come directly from Rodin's studio. With the addition of more than thirty original plaster casts, the Spreckels collection remains one of the largest in this country.

Alma de Bretteville Spreckels' death in 1968 marked a turning point in the history of the two museums. In 1970, their boards of directors agreed that their common purposes could be achieved more efficiently as one institution.

Note:

What next?

San Francisco is not only a city of superlatives, but also a hub from which one can depart in any direction and extend the excitement: west to Hawaii; north to the Redwoods, the Oregon coast, the Columbia River and Puget Sound; south to Carmel, Monterey, the Big Sur Highway, San Diego, and Baja California, Mexico; east to Virginia City, Lake Tahoe, Mammoth ski slopes, and Yosemite. (And a lot further east, fifty miles beyond Mount Rushmore at Wall, South Dakota, is the most famous drug store in the world: Ted and Dorothy Hustead's demonstration of what free ice- water can do to turn badlands into goodlands.

Photo courtesy of the Monterey Bay Aquarium

27

Monterey Bay Aquarium

On October 20, 1984, the fish came back to Monterey's historic Cannery Row.

They came back in style, too, as the stars of the now world-acclaimed Monterey Bay Aquarium. More than 6,000 creatures representing nearly 600 species fill twenty-three major galleries and some 100 exhibits.

But "aquarium" is not an adequate word. This place is a scuba-dive without an aqua-lung. It's a beach stroll among tide-pools. It is Monterey Bay in a capsule—brought to dry land for your convenience. Here, you are eyeball to eyeball with ocean critters. (They think you look funny, too.)

Sea otters frolic in an innovative two-story exhibit where you can watch them showing off above and below water. The 28-foot-high towering Kelp Forest is the world's tallest aquarium exhibit. It gives visitors a diver's-eye view of a living kelp community. It's seaweed made lovable.

Kids and adults can pet bat rays in the Bat Ray Pool, starfish, chitons and abalone in the Touch Tide Pool, or decorator crabs in the Kelp Lab. You can stroll through an open-air shore-birds aviary or beneath life-size whale models.

Microscopes, magnifiers, telescopes and even a viewer-guided underwater video camera bring visitors closer to the mysterious world beyond the aquarium's decks.

Other unique exhibits include a cylindrical display of schooling anchovies, and a diver talking with the audience through a two-way communications mask.

This bay is, of itself, the ultimate aquarium. Nature was the architect. Here along the Central California Coast is an ocean canyon nearly two miles deep. Its latitude and water temperature are just right for the ocean currents to stir up a tasty dish for the marine food chain. Big fish find the right size little fish—little fish grown fat from the nutrients that well up from deep down. This canyon is an underwater mixing bowl. All the weird and wonderful salt-water creatures get a healthy meal.

The Aquarium offers an expertly-designed "undersea tour" of Monterey Bay's hidden world. From sandy seafloors to deep granite reefs, shale shelfs, sloughs and kelp forests; the bay shelters an amazing range of habitats for sea life.

And now it's all on display where we can see it without diving or getting the bends. John Steinbeck sure wouldn't believe his eyes if he beheld Cannery Row, circa 1990.

Four marine biologists at Stanford University's Hopkins Marine Station first proposed the aquarium in 1977. Shortly thereafter they formed the non-profit Monterey Bay Aquarium Foundation. Steinbeck would be proud of this team.

Three of the biologists belonged to a family whose super-smart daddy had a mountain of discretionary spending money—and a mountain of money is what was needed. David Packard, like Rockefeller and Ford and Carnegie, happened into an era just as the door was ready to spring open—Hi-Tech this time. Packard had the vision. He became the granddaddy of Silicon Valley. With two daughters and a son-in-law immersed in the marine sciences, David and Lucille Packard were a soft touch for the $50 million needed to create the Monterey Bay Aquarium.

The design intentionally preserves the historic flavor of Cannery Row and the old Hovden Cannery that inspired it. Several parts of this abandoned cannery were restored for use or display, including the old boilers. But the Aquarium itself is state-of-the-art, attuned to new-age environment and ecology. David Packard not only played financial angel, he became a participant. He designed the machinery which simulates the surge of ocean swells rushing against a rocky shoreline; also applied a hands-on role with marine sciences in general.

Julie Packard, a daughter and now Executive Director, has been a guiding light from the inception of the project. It is the public's good fortune that she chose California's University of Santa Cruz for her graduate studies in science. From here it was a natural that she would encounter the marine biology world and connect her father to the vision of a world-class aquarium. Of such happenstances are great legacies born.

About 1.7 million people visit the 216,000-square-foot aquarium annually. And even for those who return often, something new is always underway.

The aquarium has a large staff, requires boatloads of money and welcomes contributions. When you visit here, take a sea otter to dinner. Makes them happy. Their feeding time is posted, they are voracious eaters, and they'll flip out when you pick up the check.

BALBOA PARK, CITY OF SAN DIEGO

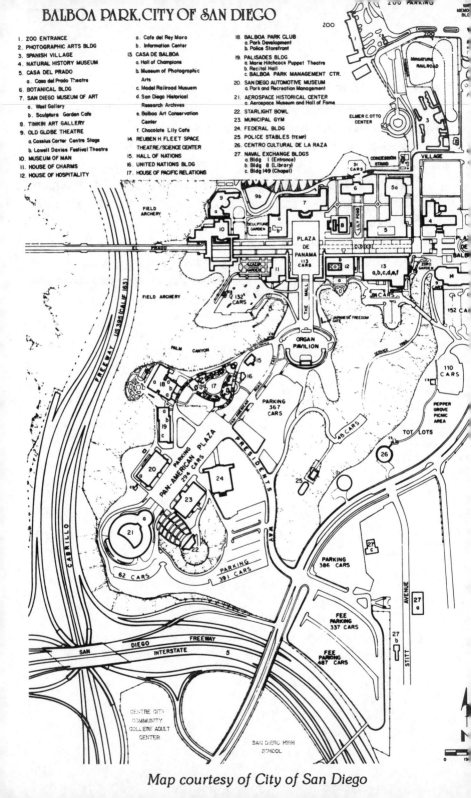

1. ZOO ENTRANCE
2. PHOTOGRAPHIC ARTS BLDG
3. SPANISH VILLAGE
4. NATURAL HISTORY MUSEUM
5. CASA DEL PRADO
   a. Casa del Prado Theatre
6. BOTANICAL BLDG
7. SAN DIEGO MUSEUM OF ART
   a. West Gallery
   b. Sculpture Garden Cafe
8. TIMKIN ART GALLERY
9. OLD GLOBE THEATRE
   a. Cassius Carter Centre Stage
   b. Lowell Davies Festival Theatre
10. MUSEUM OF MAN
11. HOUSE OF CHARMS
12. HOUSE OF HOSPITALITY

a. Cafe del Rey Moro
b. Information Center
13. CASA DE BALBOA
   a. Hall of Champions
   b. Museum of Photographic Arts
   c. Model Railroad Museum
   d. San Diego Historical Research Archives
   e. Balboa Art Conservation Center
   f. Chocolate Lily Cafe
14. REUBEN H. FLEET SPACE THEATRE/SCIENCE CENTER
15. HALL OF NATIONS
16. UNITED NATIONS BLDG
17. HOUSE OF PACIFIC RELATIONS

18. BALBOA PARK CLUB
   a. Park Development
   b. Police Storefront
19. PALISADES BLDG
   a. Marie Hitchcock Puppet Theatre
   b. Recital Hall
   c. BALBOA PARK MANAGEMENT CTR.
20. SAN DIEGO AUTOMOTIVE MUSEUM
   a. Park and Recreation Management
21. AEROSPACE HISTORICAL CENTER
   a. Aerospace Museum and Hall of Fame
22. STARLIGHT BOWL
23. MUNICIPAL GYM
24. FEDERAL BLDG
25. POLICE STABLES (TEMP)
26. CENTRO CULTURAL DE LA RAZA
27. NAVAL EXCHANGE BLDGS
   a. Bldg 1 (Entrance)
   b. Bldg 8 (Library)
   c. Bldg 149 (Chapel)

Map courtesy of City of San Diego

28

Balboa Park

Four hundred years ago, a Renaissance poet wrote, "The good Florentine is found in the square of his city, for there all manner of things happen and all manner of people pass." Today, the poet would feel very much at home in San Diego's Balboa Park.

Like the poet's square, this 1,400-acre park pulsates with vitality and life. Here are also quiet places where the harried city-dweller can find solace. Action, but also if you prefer, challenges to the mind and sustenance for the soul. No other park, including Central or Golden Gate, has such a cornucopia of museums and theater, flora and fauna. Only in Balboa Park can the words of Shakespeare and the roar of a lion share a summer evening.

Balboa Park is theater. It has been said that theater requires three things: the play, the actors and the audience—and each must give something. Many San Diegans loyally buy season tickets and Balboa Park's theaters return that love with superb plays and musicals. Michael McKeever, author of A Short History of San Diego, described Balboa Park:

"Five park theaters offer a buffet for every taste from classical to experimental to bright musicals. On warm summer evenings, audiences in the open-air Starlight Bowl enjoy musicals on a stage large enough for even the Music Man and all 76 of his trombones.

"Across the park, the Old Globe Theatre rings with the words of Shakespeare. Next to the Old Globe is the intimate Cassius Carter Centre Stage, with its 'theater-in-the-round.' Just beyond that, nestled in a grove of trees, is the park's newest, the Lowell Davies Festival Theatre."

Great parks are not built; they are lovingly nurtured and sculpted throughout the decades. For Balboa Park, the journey from neglected playground to "cultural heart of San Diego" began in 1868, the year San Diego's leaders set aside 1,400 acres for a city park. Occasionally a civic group would plant a few bushes and many San Diegans found the park's canyons made fine dumping grounds. But otherwise, the site was virtually ignored for almost a quarter of a century. Then in 1892, the city struck an extraordinary bargain with Kate Sessions that allowed her to operate a private nursery on park land. What was so extraordinary about the deal? Sessions' rent was to be paid in trees, not cash! For the next decade, Sessions planted at least 100 trees a year in the park, as well as another 300 throughout the city. By the turn of the century, Balboa Park was a horticulture wonderland.

As the park evolved, a fitting name was needed, so a contest was held. One entry pointed out that since the park offered a sweeping view of the Pacific Ocean, it might be proper to honor the Spanish explorer who first sighted the Pacific, and the park was christened "Balboa." About that time, 1915, the Panama Canal was nearing its completion. Why not, then, hold a grand international exposition in its honor? In San Francisco, a rival "official" exposition was also planned, but San Diego felt there was room for two. Thus, the Panama-California Exposition was vivified. An elegant little city rose on the top of dry hills. On January 1, 1915, the Panama-California Exposition opened its doors.

In the closing months of the exposition, one of those wonderful incidents happened that become part of a city's folklore. In late 1916, a local doctor was driving past the exposition grounds when he heard the roar of a lion, the orphan of a temporary zoo. Dr. Harry Wegeforth thought it would be a splendid idea for San Diego to have a permanent zoo. Soon Wegeforth put together a patchwork collection of animals gathered from wherever he could get them. Some were leftovers from the exposition, others were donated pets or mascots. At first, the animals were housed in ramshackle wood-and-wire cages along Park Boulevard. Today, the San Diego Zoo, born of a passing thought, is one of the great zoos of the world.

It was in the gray depths of the Great Depression that Balboa Park saw its second exposition—the California-Pacific International. Like the 1915 exposition, the 1935-36 spectacle offered a wide choice of delights—Old Globe Theatre, for example, presented 45-minute segments of Shakespeare. People wanted to escape, to enjoy, to be amazed. Alpha the Robot shook hands and talked in a mechanical voice. Zorine the Nudist Queen cavorted with her court in a leafy glade. One could (and did) see everything from Shirley Temple shows to Sally Rand. And, for a few months, the depression seemed a little easier to bear.

When Pearl Harbor was bombed, Balboa Park went to war. Except for the zoo, it became a vast extension of the Navy Hospital. Wounded were moved into the museums. The Ford Building (today's Aerospace Museum) rang with the sound of aircraft assemblers learning to weld. A vast horde of war-service Americans were moved through San Diego or stationed there. It was inevitable they would note the great climate, bluffs and beaches, and many would migrate there. The city grew—as did Balboa Park—with the Museum of Photographic Arts, the Hall of Champions, which honors the strength and courage of San Diego athletes, the San Diego Historical Society's Research Archives, and the Aerospace Museum, which displays planes that carried us aloft in war and peace, their engines silent now except in the imaginations of thousands of visitors.

In the Natural History Museum, our world—from dinosaur to seismography—is on display. Across the plaza, with its inviting fountain, is the Reuben H. Fleet Space Theater and Science Center, where audiences can watch the eternity of the cosmos beneath the planetarium dome. Sharing the Space Theater building is the Science Center, where velvet ropes and "do not disturb" signs are delightfully absent. Visitors are actually invited to be part of the exhibits through a series of unique demonstrations. Down the Prado stands the Botanical Building. Inside its cool shade, a lush, ever-changing plethora of flowers and trees thrives with tender care. The botanical and horticultural attractions deserve as much attention as do the animals. But centerstage is the ZOO. Spread over 100 acres of mesas and winding canyons, the zoo has been a parkgoer's delight for almost three-quarters of a century. With thousands of animals and plants in their native environments, it is far more than a day's entertainment. Indeed, it's a fifty-kilometer drive to the country to see the rest: the Wild Animal Park. It is, for many species, a Noah's Ark, a last hope for those who stand in the shadow of extinction.

Balboa Park is far more than beautifully-housed exhibits. It is the laughter of children playing among the branches of a massive Australian fig tree and the quiet murmur of couples strolling in the peace of a palm canyon. It is picnics on the lawn and tennis and lawn bowling. It is lying on soft green grass on a sunny day listening to the birds, feeling the peace and beauty generations of caring people have created for all of us.

Virtually every community in the United States boasts a city park, but the truly great parks can be counted on one hand. San Diego's Balboa Park is one of that elite handful. Larger than New York's Central Park and older than San Francisco's Golden Gate Park, Balboa Park is the "cultural heart of San Diego."

Photo courtesy of Hotel del Coronado

29

The del Coronado

Drive toward the setting sun as you leave Balboa Park, and you'll cross a bridge that's really something to tell the folks back home about. From its apogee, look ahead to the Pacific Ocean to see a structure resembling a . . . well, it's hard to describe, but it's the Hotel del Coronado.

Whatever you wish to call the hotel's architecture, it is extravagant and it beckons. A monument to the past—with turrets and cupolas, hand-carved pillars and Victorian gingerbread—it is in the National Register of Historic Places, naturally. Opened in 1888, this centenarian belongs in Willard Scott's exclusive club.

When the Del opened, San Diego was a small, ho-hum Pacific port, and the Coronado Peninsula was a vacant sandspit. Elisha Babcock and H.L. Story purchased 4,100 acres of wasteland for $27 an acre. These days, that $110,000 would barely cover the down payment on an ocean-facing condo adjacent to the hotel.

Babcock was a railroad tycoon with the crazy dream of building a resort that would be the "talk of the western world" at a time when the American West was still untamed, when many of the workmen were unskilled Chinese laborers, when lumber came by ship from northern California.

A project ahead of its time, the del Coronado Hotel was the largest structure outside the city of New York to use electric lighting. Thomas Edison supervised the installation of his incandescent lamps and a few years later in 1904 he pulled the switch on the hotel's first electrically-lighted Christmas tree.

For opening day, thousands of spectators traveled from across the United States to this unusual structure. The hotel gradually established itself as a cultural oasis for European charm and cuisine, and Babcock's dream grew bigger than life.

The hotel has hosted twelve U.S. presidents and an endless

stream of other dignitaries. The Prince of Wales, for whom special china trimmed in gold was created, met commoner Wally Simpson there and later abdicated his throne to marry her. Regular guests included show business greats: Burt Bacharach, John Wayne, Bob Newhart, Pearl Bailey and Lucille Ball; also the Astors, Vanderbilts, Tiffanys and Armours.

Although some structural changes have been made over the years, many of the original facilities are still available. For instance, the Crown Room, which easily seats 1,000 people, is virtually the same as the day it was built. The arched ceiling of natural-finished sugar-pine fitted together with pegs (no nails) has a unique support system in which no posts or other interior supports are required. The Grand Ballroom, with enormous chandeliers hung from the 31-foot ceiling, overlooks the ocean and is a super setting for a gala function such as your next anniversary, if you have a thousand friends to impress and a big budget.

On September 21, 1927, the del Coronado was the site of a dinner honoring Charles Lindbergh, following his solo flight over the Atlantic. What better place, since his Spirit of St. Louis was built across the bay at San Diego.

A familiar sight to movie and television audiences, this grand hotel is one of Hollywood's most popular filming locations. Marilyn Monroe was an honored guest when the Del served as the primary setting for Billy Wilder's 1950s film hit, Some Like It Hot, with Jack Lemmon and Tony Curtis. The Academy-Award-nominated movie The Stunt Man, starring Peter O'Toole, also featured the del Coronado in part of its production, and it served as the inspiration for Somewhere in Time.

It is said that L. Frank Baum, author of The Wizard of Oz, based the design of his Emerald City on the Coronado hotel. The Del was immensely popular as a television setting as well in such productions as Hart to Hart and Simon and Simon.

Combine the del Coronado's illustrious history and its proximity to Hollywood with one of the best warm-weather climates in the U.S., and it is understandable why Rand McNally's 1986 edition claimed that it " . . . enjoys more fame and historical significance than perhaps any other hotel in North America."

The Hotel del Coronado is a modernized antique. It opened for guests at a time when Ford's Model T couldn't outrun a horse, and it still struts in an age when men and women orbit the earth in seventy-two minutes. When you tell your friends about your visit, you may borrow my line: "It's a hotel I can't quite describe—and I love it!" (. . . and that's why it's on the cover . . .)

"I've put the sweat of my life into this thing. I have my reputation rolled up in it. I have stated several times, if it's a failure I'll probably leave this country and never come back."

Howard Robard Hughes
August 1947

LONGER THAN A FOOTBALL FIELD — With a wingspan more than 319 feet — larger than a football field — Howard Hughes' "Spruce Goose" perches in its permanent resting place inside the world's largest clear-span aluminum dome beside the regal Queen Mary in Long Beach, Calif. The legendary aircraft, which was hidden in a temperature-controlled hangar following its one-and-only flight on Nov. 2, 1947, is open for public viewing for the first time in more than 30 years. The spectacular Spruce Goose exhibit features the 400,000-pound, all-wood flying boat as its center piece, surrounded by a permanent display of aviation artifacts and memorabilia of Howard Hughes' aviation and film careers. The Spruce Goose exhibit, located on Pier J in the

30

Spruce Goose
Howard Hughes

It was the early thirties and the film, *Hell's Angels*, was electrifying the entertainment industry. Howard Hughes' start in the movie world had been mediocre at best, and such was not Hughes' grand plan. Once and for all he wanted to convince the world that he was a master movie maker.

It needed only a sensual blonde to convince me. At age fourteen I neither knew nor cared who the the producer was (Hughes), who the director was (Hughes), or who laid out the biggest bundle of money ever for a movie (Hughes—$3.8 million). Jean Harlow's cleavage sent a message from the silver screen, and this bug-eyed boy in the 10-cent movie house was jolted toward puberty.

For "Hell's Angels," Hughes scoured two continents to locate eighty-seven World War I vintage aircraft. He put them in flying condition. He recruited 137 aviators and stunt flyers. He was at that time the commander of the world's largest private air force.

Hughes ignored cost to portray reality. The dogfights were real, the suspense was real, the love-intrigue was real, and Jean Harlow, in her first starring role, was so real that women across the country rushed to the beauty parlors to bleach their hair blonde. Did the movie-going public ever get its money's worth!

"Billionaire" was once the sound barrier of wealth. Hughes may have been the first U.S. enterpriser to pierce that barrier. If not the first, he was certainly the youngest. What did it take? Genius? Imagination? Drive and motivation? All these and lots of luck! In Hughes' case, luck meant having a father to bequeath to him, at age eighteen, 75% of the Hughes Tool Company. Howard Robard Hughes, Jr. was able to hit the ground running. He was the only son of a daddy who had been in the right spot (Texas) at the right time (new oil) with the right idea (a drill bit that could chew through rock). And for future movie-making, it certainly helped to have an uncle (Rupert Hughes) who was a successful screenwriter for Samuel Goldwyn, which gave easy access to the glitter and glamour of the Hollywood lifestyle.

Luck he had, and lots of it, but the Hughes career was also littered with bad calls (he turned down James Cagney and Clark Gable), near-misses with death (usually plane crashes), bad marriages (several), and associates who couldn't function with such an introverted eccentric. With enough wealth to absorb wild risks out of his petty cash, he soared from mystery to headline, fact to fancy, intrigue to legend.

Aviation was a consuming passion with Howard Hughes. He loved it even to going undercover to fly co-pilot with American Airways. Under the pseudonym Charles Howard, he first flew Fokker tri-motor transports, then later DC-2's for TWA. He liked planes and he liked them fast.

Hughes pioneered transcontinental routes and set numerous speed records, including a transatlantic crossing in one-half Lindbergh's time. His record flight around the world in just ninety-one hours earned him a ticker-tape parade down Broadway.

Ever impatient to stay in the vanguard of aeronautical development, he tried repeatedly to be part of the World War II drama. Herein lies our monument to Howard Hughes:

THE HUGHES FLYING BOAT—nicknamed "The Spruce Goose"—began with a bright idea by Henry Kaiser, the Liberty Ship king. World War II's Achilles heel was cargo shipping. Kaiser rode to the rescue with mass-produced liberty ships. Even so, the Germans sank them as fast as Kaiser's yards could launch them. Out of desperation was born inspiration. "Why not put wings on ships?" Kaiser pondered. This idea was too incredible to receive much of an audience, but Kaiser persisted and sought aeronautical expertise. Hughes was the only expert wild enough to undertake such a crazy scheme. After all, it was to be constructed of wood! The aircraft community figured it was impossible, and that was bait enough. Howard Hughes was hooked. He went it alone. It was his baby.

Hughes moved in a cloud of secrecy. Little or nothing was

known about the progress, viability or cost of the Spruce Goose. Congress chided him for wasting money, critics jeered, and believers were scarce. Yet there came a day. Santa Barbara writer Cork Millner tells it thus:

"Howard Hughes eased his lean frame into the seat behind the pilot's console, took off his favorite brown fedora and put on earphones. As he grasped the throttles that controlled the huge Flying Boat's eight engines, he smiled at Dave Grant, the hydraulic engineer sitting in the copilot's seat. Today is the day, the smile said—today is the day!

No one thought the Howard Hughes Flying Boat would ever get into the air. Hughes had been accused of building a flying lumber yard, a "spruce goose" that was far too massive to lift itself skyward. It weighed 400,000 pounds, had eight Pratt & Whitney engines, a vertical tail as tall as an eight-story building and a wingspan of 320 feet. The Wright brothers' famous Kitty Hawk could have taken off from one wingtip and landed before reaching the hull. Even Hughes entertained some doubts about his creation's ability to fly.

"I have put the sweat of my life into this thing," he said. "I have my reputation rolled up into it. If it's a failure I'll probably leave this country and never come back."

Whether the great airplane would be Hughes' watery tomb or his lasting memorial was going to be decided this day, November 2, 1947.

Hughes pushed forward on the throttles and the Flying Boat pulled away from the Long Beach harbor, then picked up speed to 35 miles per hour. Hughes tested the controls. The hydraulics were functioning normally. After this first slow speed run, Hughes turned to the six members of the press he had allowed aboard and said, "Better hold on tight because we're really going to pick up speed on this run." The giant seaplane accelerated, seventy miles per hour . . . ninety . . . the choppy waves beat a staccato of sound against the wooden hull. Then, as the forward portion of the hull lifted clear of water, Hughes retarded the throttles and the mammoth craft slowed. The reporters sighed in relief. Hughes had told them he was only going to conduct taxi tests; the first flight wouldn't come for several months.

With the exception of radio newsman Jimmy McNamara, Hughes disembarked the reporters, then turned to his copilot, Dave Grant, and said, "Flaps, fifteen degrees." Grant's eyes widened. This was the takeoff setting for the Flying Boat.

News reporter Jimmy McNamara looked over Hughes' shoulder and, as the millionaire pilot eased the throttles forward, broadcast what happened: "We're at forty miles per hour, over a choppy sea . . . more throttle, fifty-five miles per hour . . . more throttle . . . " McNamara pressed his lips tightly to his microphone to be heard over the screaming protest of the engines and the pounding of whitecaps against the hull. His voice rose in pitch . . . what was Hughes doing? "Sixty-five miles per hour . . . seventy . . . !"

Then . . . silence.

The beat of the waves against the hull was gone, the pounding of the engines reduced to a muted hum. There was only the whistling of the air as the great plane hung suspended for a moment in time and space."

Barely one mile . . . but it was a flight. Too late for proving any viability for the war which was now over. The Spruce Goose went undercover into an extravagant hangar for three decades. A $25 million exile, hiding from scrutiny.

With the passage of time, Hughes became obsessed with privacy, and we know very little of the man's later years. He created no monument to himself, built no mansion unless a dozen Las Vegas casinos qualify. In 1953 he did create a Foundation, maybe to avoid taxes. It took on a size to top the big-league givers, and its purpose was noble. The Howard Hughes Medical Institute is probably benefitting a host of the living but, like Hughes, it seems to be nearly invisible.

If Hughes deserved a memorial, someone else would have to do it for him . . . but *what* and *how*, and did anyone care?

When Hughes died, the $1-million-per-year cost of keeping the Spruce Goose in mothballs was determined an unacceptable expense in the eyes of the court. The judge ruled that it must go to the boneyard. It was on death row when hotelier Jack Wrather stepped forward and offered a plan and money to enshrine the world's largest airplane alongside the world's largest ocean liner. As with the Queen Mary, moving and housing the monster presented monster-size problems. These were surmounted, and in 1983, seven years after Hughes' death, the Spruce Goose was on public display—floating proudly on the water of an artificial bay within the largest clear-span aluminum dome in the world.

Visitors to this aeronautical wonder of the world actually enter the plane's massive cargo hold to view its interior, a cavern designed to carry 750 combat-ready troops, or a pair of 30-ton Sherman tanks. Viewing platforms allow guests to look into the flying boat's flight deck. There sits a mannequin wearing Hughes' stoic expression, topped by his brown fedora.

Surrounding the plane are a variety of fascinating displays telling the story of the design, construction and its one-and-only flight. Many of Hughes' personal and aviation artifacts are displayed, and there is a full-scale replica of his first racing plane, also an actual Sherman tank.

Hughes' sentiment written on a 1947 photo of the first and only flight is now more than just wishful thinking:

> "I hope someday Long Beach will regard this plane
> with a certain amount of pride."

Howard Hughes' flying career put his life on the line innumerable times, but always as the pilot in command. What irony that his life ended as a passenger aboard a safe, albeit final flight, April 5, 1976.

The Queen Mary Hotel

Throughout this book, whenever we know a nearby hotel that belongs in the same league as the attraction, we ask you to trust us. By staying at the Spruce Goose, we propose that you can literally enlarge the experience. Consider: the world's biggest cargo plane that will never fly again hangared beside the world's biggest passenger ship that will never sail again.

The Queen Mary Hotel belongs in the Disney wonderworld—and that's who manages it—finally. This monster was not easy for Long Beach to digest. When the ship went up for grabs, the City of Long Beach took a long gamble. There were rough seas for planning and for the budget. Numerous Long Beach boosters tugged at the hawsers before this leviathan was beached. Jack Wrather got into the act, which was good training for his future tussle with the Spruce Goose. Somehow things fell into place, and today the Queen is securely docked at Pier J, Port of Long Beach.

Register for the night; dine with the captain. If there's an easier way to cruise on a ship that holds most of the world's records, tell this writer about it. No seasickness, no budget-busting, no waiting in line for the all-ashore launch, and no customs.

Pinkie, by Sir Thomas Lawrence, 1794

*Blue Boy, by Thomas
Gainsborough (c.1770)*

*The Gutenberg Bible
(c.1455)*

Photos this page courtesy of the Huntington Library

31

Huntington and His Library

Los Angeles needs this industrialist back, and for a critical reason. For more books? No. Of course, books are important, but the real need is to solve the problem that most often characterizes L.A.: traffic and its smog. This is a story about the master of mass transit, the organizer of the now-extinct L.A. Railway system.

Henry Edwards Huntington lived an Horatio Alger story. Born in Oneonta, New York, in 1850, he plunged into the business world at a time when the work ethic was in. His playmates in school knew, "You can't get ahead of Ed Huntington." Early in life, hard work put this young entrepreneur on a roll. Of course, having an uncle named Collis P. Huntington was certainly a lucky catapult. Collis was a railroad baron. He recognized his nephew as a strong manager-type and made him part of an already vast business empire. In 1892, C.P. brought his nephew to San Francisco to share in the management of the Southern Pacific Railroad.

San Francisco's electric railways grabbed H.E., and sometime around 1902 he shifted to Los Angeles where he created an interurban system surpassing anything of its kind hitherto known. Nowadays it is hard to believe that there was once a time when getting from one end of L.A. to the other was as easy as boarding one of the "big red cars." That system is now gone, and L.A. commuters in their stalled traffic or inching their way across Sepulveda Pass on the freeway, might well pray for a reincarnation of Henry E. Huntington . . . for appointment to Cal Trans.

Early in this century, Henry Huntington made frequent business trips east (Newport News Shipbuilding was a Huntington property), and during these times bought heavily into books, manuscripts and art. It became evident he was a born collector with an instinctive appreciation of art and literature. Huntington's acquisitions became so extensive that he had no place to store them in his New York residence. The solution lay across the continent at San Marino Ranch.

In 1892, while moving at uncle's request from the east coast to the west, H.E. stopped over in Los Angeles and, as fate willed it, was entertained by J. de Barth Shorb at "San Marino" estate. Unknown to Huntington, he was standing on the choice parcel of earth that he would later own. Initially it was 550 acres (imagine—nearly a square mile between Pasadena and L.A.!). It would in time be reduced to 207. Henry bought the property after Uncle Collis died in 1900 and left his nephew a large legacy. Said nephew was already doing famously and was deeply involved in the phenomenal development of California. In time, Huntington would serve on as many as sixty company boards throughout the United States.

In 1906 Mr. Huntington commissioned two architects, Myron Hunt and Elmer Grey, to design housing for his family and also for his art and literary collections.

His monument was sited. There would soon evolve a library of world renown, an art gallery and a botanical garden. It would also set the standard for the incorporated community which now surrounds it—a pride-of-ownership neighborhood, famous for its orderly beauty. When you drive about San Marino you will surely agree.

With more money than he needed, Mr. Huntington phased out of his work-saga at around age sixty and switched to his new dedication. Those who knew him suspected that retirement would unleash pursuits more noble than material success. He became a collector-in-a-hurry, and to this he applied his business acumen. He bought entire private collections, paying whatever the auction demanded, and in 1911 he breached the million-dollar barrier with his bid for the Dwight Church book collection. This one added 2133 rare editions and marked him as a collector to be reckoned with ($1 million in 1911 converts to around $49 million in 1990 purchasing power). Shortly thereafter he outbid the room for a Gutenberg Bible, one of twelve surviving copies printed on vellum (the inner skin of a sheep or calf). His purchase of entire libraries continued unabated. In a relatively short time, Mr. Huntington was acknowledged to be the outstanding book collector in the U.S., possibly in the world. Only ten years earlier his name had not even been entered in a New York survey of private libraries. An educated guess by the New York Times in 1917 stated that Hungtington had spent six million on his library in six years. By this time, most of it was housed in the new structure at San Marino.

By 1919 Mr. Huntington's monument had grown too vast for private containment, so he created a trust to open this rich legacy to the public. An endowment was provided which now funds about 60% of the operating budget. The rest derives from donations and other outside sources. The paid staff now number about 210. There are over 400 trained volunteers.

Thus it happens that you and I and our heirs can stroll through the great exhibition hall and view the *Gutenberg Bible*, Chaucer's *Canterbury Tales*, Audubon's *Birds of America*, and thousands of other original works of literature and art. We can gaze upon Gainsborough's *The Blue Boy* and Lawrence's *Pinkie*. We can stroll through 150 acres of botanical gardens. It is an endless feast for the senses.

Today the Huntington is one of the great research libraries of the world. The collections contain 2.2 million manuscripts, 336,000 rare books and a quarter-million reference books concentrated in the fields of British and American history.

Driving instructions: The Huntington Library is easily accessible by our favorite route: use the Foothill Freeway (either East or West 210), exit to Sierra Madre Boulevard and follow it south through Pasadena. After a few signal lights you will see a "San Marino" marker that tells your eyes you've entered a special municipality of prideful homes. Turn right on Los Robles and . . . well, there are several routes. (We happened to pick this one because it leads past a home once occupied by our daughter and her family.) There are lots of signs to guide you. Check the Appendix for operating hours and so forth.

Doors of San Sylmar
Photo courtesy of Merle Norman Cosmetics

32

San Sylmar

"San Sylmar? Where's that?"

I explain, "At Sylmar. Same place that gave its name to an earthquake that did a lot of mischief in 1971 . . . ."

"Oh, that place."

How very many times have I tried to open the eyes of my California friends to the wonder of a crown jewel right in Los Angeles' backyard (or front, depending on your direction of travel). Sylmar, at the north end of the San Fernando Valley, gets lost in the maze of faceless communities that make up the megalopolis.

The "San Sylmar Classic Beauty Collection," established by Merle Norman, deserves to be on a pedestal. Maybe on a mountain top like the Hearst Castle. For reasons best known to its creator, this attraction is housed in a non-period structure located in a humble neighborhood on the wrong side of the nearby tracks. Its construction coincided with the earthquake. And why not? To be in coastal California means to live astride a fault. The new structure suffered some damage but recovered, and for that is the more cherished.

As you wait to be admitted, you may be puzzled that two ornate doors (1500 pounds of pure artistry) are the only evidence that this is a special place. The stark exterior with neither sign nor adornment belies the breathtaking beauty concealed behind the windowless walls. As you pass from a drab industrial street into this shrine, your reaction is apt to be culture shock. You gasp, "Rolls Royces! Wall to wall!" Next, up a level to the Grand Salon, showcase for J.B. Nethercutt's collage of vintage classic autos. About thirty are on display. They glisten, they speak of great personages, they rouse memories, they generate lust. They are all operable and another one hundred or more are stabled elsewhere, waiting to join this revolving display.

These jewels are not cordoned off. Viewers are allowed to

circulate in groups of fifty or so. One notes the reluctance of any person to touch. Not even a clod would think of leaving a fingerprint on one of these shiny chariots.

A grand staircase brings visitors to another Merle Norman surprise: "Cloud Ninety-Nine." Another gasp! A plush assembly area for the world's largest collection of mechanical music makers. Big and small, they all play. As they give forth their distinctive tones, one hears melodies and compositions preserved from entertainments of long ago. These handsome cabinets have within them the music of the ages, and a push of the button releases it, filling the room. The centerpiece of this great room is a mighty 1926 Wurlitzer Theatre Pipe Organ. The console rises above the floor, and 2500 pipes resound. The hi-tech magic of our modern era can play back from its own computer the performance of contemporary masters who come here to record and share their talent with visitors to "Cloud 99!"

The San Sylmar Classic Beauty Collection is one very unique treasure house. It is something you definitely want to see. Trust me. And the price is right. It's free! Can you believe, it all started with makeup?

Merle Norman opened her first cosmetic studio in 1931, and was soon joined by her nephew, J.B. Nethercutt. Together they launched the company that has probably put more women in business than any other venture. Merle Norman retired in 1963, and her nephew has held the course. This amazing attraction is a joint tribute to these two entrepreneurs.

Mr. Nethercutt's guide emphasizes that the artisans whose handiwork made this possible were found in Southern California. The autos run, the music devices play—good to hear there are still skilled workers on the local turf who know their craft.

San Sylmar requires advance reservations for specific admitting time. This complicates it for tourists, as there always seems to be a backlog. Visitors are conducted in groups. There is a dress code (no blue jeans, shorts or halter tops). Children under thirteen are not admitted (for good reason). The appointment times are precise, so allow extra time for L.A. traffic. (There is no public transportation that a stranger can endure.)

The San Sylmar tours are timed to allow noon hour lunch—either before or after. There is a well-worn route, by vehicle, to and from The Odyssey, a popular watering-hole in nearby Granada Hills with a great view overlooking the San Fernando Valley. This restaurant is accessible from Rinaldi, but a stranger had best get on-the-spot directions. Phone number is in the Appendix. Do it! Eating at The Odyssey will frost your cake.

The House On The Rock!

The musical devices at San Sylmar are experienced on thick carpet, surrounded by elegance, and inspire deep appreciation. For contrast, back in Wisconsin, west of Madison, the House on the Rock provides the outlandish! Alex Jordan has assembled in his spectacle—his citadel—his psychadelic whatzit (there is no suitable word)—a dozen animated, automated, orchestrated music-makers. In the sequel to this book, an attempt will be made to describe this madcap conglomerate. If you're anywhere near Wisconsin, make the effort. Allow two or three hours and brace yourself for a treat!

Photo courtesy of The J. Paul Getty Museum
Julius Shulman, photographer

33

The Getty Museum

Aphrodite, goddess of love, is home again—at Mount Olympus West, otherwise known as Malibu on the Pacific. This $20-million sculpture is enshrined in surroundings as similar to her home in Southern Italy as her creator, 2500 years ago, could ever have hoped. John Paul Getty's replica of the Villa dei Papiri has an elegance early Romans could only have dreamed of.

Herculaneum, the ancient city, shared the same fate as Pompeii when Vesuvius turned its neighborhood into a crematorium. That was A.D. 79. Entombed until the 18th century, it was finally exposed to daylight about 1828, much better preserved than Pompeii.

Getty first visited Herculaneum and the Villa of the Papyri as a twenty-year-old, and resolved to recreate it, when maturity and money permitted, on his estate in California. It would be a showcase for his ever-expanding art collection. Because the statue of Aphrodite survived intact for 2000 years, all 7½ feet from head to toe, it is unique and special. Little wonder that Getty's museum has earthquake-proofed this 1000-pound statue. The goddess of love can now ride out a quake of eight on the Richter scale and maybe even cause one! Who knows what these Greek goddesses can do if spurned or provoked?

Here's some fateful symbolism: Aphrodite and Getty, two paramours of legend! Not since she wheedled Paris out of the golden apple has her potent spell been more amorous than with J.P. Getty. Getty was a ladies' man with five wives and five divorces, solicited by Playboy Magazine for his wisdom.

For his museum, Mr. Getty chose a narrow valley descending to the sea. Unfortunately, a very busy Pacific Coast Highway now isolates this extraordinary attraction from a very appealing ocean beach. Getty closely followed and approved every phase of the design and construction. The museum opened to the public in 1974. (See the Appendix for parking and visitor information.)

The Getty Museum has all the collectibles one would expect in an art museum, and more. It is so heavily endowed that it can offer $50 plus million for Vincent Van Gogh's *Irises* without even referring to its check register. It is not a bidder with which other museums wish to compete.

How did Getty acquire so much money? Simply lots and lots of smarts plus a rich and clever daddy. George Getty sent his Minneapolis son to Oxford, then steered him into oil. The kid's first well came in a gusher when the rest of his peers couldn't afford a used Model T. Barely into his twenties, and already a millionaire, J.P. decided to retire while his depression-bound peers wondered where to find jobs washing dishes.

When son Paul inherited his daddy's whole kaboodle and had to go to work, the question was what to do with a company worth $10-15 million depression era dollars? (That converts to roughly half a billion modern-day dollars.) This fortune was quite liquid at a time when the rest of the country was being foreclosed or was jumping out of office windows. Young Getty attended fire sales and bought distressed property and securities with the scarcest commodity on the street: cash!

Liquidity also served him well in the art world. The 1929 stock market crash brought a lot of choice masterpieces out of hiding to exchange for carfare out of town. In Getty's own story *The Golden Age* (and it certainly was for him), he tells of creaming the market, paying "a minute fraction" of what previous owners had paid. For example, Getty purchased Raphael's *Madonna of Loreto* for $200.

After the depression-caused sacrifices had been skimmed off, Getty scanned Europe for liquidations induced by fear of war. He collected a mountain of art treasures.

It might be easy to envy John Paul Getty, especially the jumpstart he enjoyed as a youth, also his appreciation of art and his ability to take on foreign language.

Conversely, judging from his writings, it may be that Getty envied those of us who found a marriage relationship that was comfortable and enduring, who were spared endless litigation and proxy fights, who haven't had to retreat within a lonely castle in England—and most of all, we who can visit the Getty Museum as the donor never succeeded in doing. And that's incredible!

Mr. Getty is memorialized by the trust he created. His museum, so rich it subsidizes its competitors at art sales, is only one part of the great master plan. Soon, perhaps by 1995, the J. Paul Getty Center will combine a dozen Los Angeles-based programs and a new museum on a dramatic 110-acre hilltop site overlooking Los Angeles and the Pacific Ocean. Low-lying buildings, almost a village, will cluster along two intersecting mountain ridges. A veritable campus will include a 450-seat auditorium, visitor facilities, a six-level parking garage and an electric shuttle system. It will be a cornucopia from which grants will flow worldwide to others who share Getty's obsession with art and history. Here this billionaire's wealth will recycle back to the public domain, back to the populace, back to you and me. Mr. Getty, thumbs up!

SOLANO
SAN RAFAEL
SACRAMENTO
SAN FRANCISCO
DOLORES
SAN JOSE
SANTA CLARA
SANTA CRUZ
MONTEREY
SAN JUAN BAUTISTA
SAN CARLOS
SOLEDAD
SAN ANTONIO
SAN MIGUEL
SAN LUIS OBISPO
PURISIMA
SANTA INES
SANTA BARBARA
SANTA BARBARA
VENTURA
SAN FERNANDO
LOS ANGELES
SAN GABRIEL
SAN CAPIS
SAN DIEGO

Pacific

Nevada

34

The California Mission Trail

"God Gave Us The Country:
The Skill of Man Hath Built The Town"
—Roman motto, over an arch at
the Santa Barbara Courthouse

Between San Diego and Monterey stretches "El Camino Real," the King's Highway. It is also called Cabrillo Highway, or Pacific Coast Highway. To drive it is one of life's treats. Not so before pavement and tourist services. It was the route followed, when but a barely discernible trail, by Father Junipero Serra and his compadres. It was a long and lonely trek by foot or mule, totally lacking creature comforts. If Fr. Serra is canonized as is proposed, he will have earned it the hard way and quite belatedly. Only a saint would have sweat and shivered across the rugged California terrain for love of a rag-tag people and "God's work." The "work" was purely that, and it resulted in a string of Missions that are our legacy from those dedicated and money-poor humanitarians. If the visitor wishes to understand California history, this Mission Trail is the starting point.

There are a score of missions, and to see them all is a needless workout when a stopover at Santa Barbara permits a visit to "the queen of the missions." Here, out of the traffic congestion of San Francisco and Los Angeles, the pilgrim can find sanctuary. This mission is unique in that it has functioned continuously from its founding in 1786 up to the present. There are frequent tours guided by brown-robed Franciscan padres, and if the visitor wishes to make the experience total, services and mass adhere to traditional schedules.

Although the city's downtown architecture is uniquely Moorish-Spanish by edict, it has not always been so. It required an earthquake to inspire the citizenry to a fresh start and controlled design. Nature obliged the morning of June 29, 1925. Enough public structures, including the County Courthouse, were destroyed to trigger a restrictive ordinance. Thereafter the central district became "el Pueblo Viejo," and subsequent construction has been Moorish-Spanish, i.e., red tile roofs, balconies, galleries, wrought iron, stucco. High-rise is prohibido.

Santa Barbara's new Courthouse was to be the crown jewel of the rebuilding. Architect William Mooser, along with his son, who had seventeen years of European experience, were chosen from a competition. The winners designed a winner. Perhaps the single feature that makes the deepest impression is the supervisors' chamber with its massive mural, covering three walls and depicting California's history starting with Cabrillo's landing in 1542.

A minor problem with such a grandiose concept: the sparsely-settled county could not afford it . . . except . . . .

Of all the luck! Newly-discovered oil was just spudding in along the beach line west of town. It was ripe to be assessed for property taxes, and its first year's bill, just by coincidence,seemed to match the cost of a splendid new Courthouse. Oil was good!

Forty years later, a well in the ocean channel blew out and covered the beaches with sticky *goo*—which soon became an acronym for "Get Oil Out," the name taken by a citizen protest organization. Suddenly oil was bad!

This blowout caused an awakening for which the oil industry has paid dearly—for pollution at Santa Barbara and elsewhere. The channel is currently dotted with oil platforms; one of them is the tallest skyscraper in the world (1480 feet, of which 280 feet are visible). Oil remains an adversarial subject with Santa Barbara. Whether the visitor sees art form or ugly platforms, for the locals, oil production in all its guises is the object of a tenacious love-hate relationship.

Since visitors to this part of California may have difficulty with their direction, the topography map inside the Courthouse should merit a moment. This visual aid helps the visitor accept that the coastline here, and the Santa Ynez Mountains, run east-west, and the streets do not. This map was created by the Civilian

Conservation Corps in the depression era, a reminder that California's economic history includes "the grapes of wrath." The state has not always been all wine and roses.

If you ascend the Courthouse tower for a bird's-eye view of the city, a word of warning. It was from this high perspective, looking out over Santa Barbara's romantic vistas, that I identified my own promised land, and in time migrated to a charming city, small enough to be likable, with ideal weather and entertainment. Many others are here for similar reasons. Insignificant venturings, like a climb to admire the view, can change the course of one's life.

A world-recognized school of photography is located in Santa Barbara. Since 1945, Brooks Institute has been choosing the Courthouse and Mission as a first assignment for its students. It's hard to imagine the number of times those two attractions have been cropped and clipped and littered the dark room. It's a safe bet these two subjects have been in more view finders than any other objects on the tour trail. The pictures in this chapter are the work of Brooks students Yeui Cheol Park and Don Short.

The Saturday after the Summer Solstice is a smart time to visit Santa Barbara. That weekend you can witness a festival of creativity. It is a vigorish time when any and all, especially the young, take to the streets with dance and artistry, buffoonery, song and good feeling. It's a people event (no horses, motorized floats or bands) when marchers and spectators celebrate summer. If you prefer more structured parades, visit in early August for the Spanish "Fiesta."

On Sunday, the Domingo arts/crafts bazaar stretches for a mile along Cabrillo Boulevard, adjacent to the beach, year-round. In March there is a week-long International Film Festival. Also check with the Arlington Theatre (one of the few remaining *real* movie houses) for the lucky chance the great Morton Theatre Organ, lovingly restored, will be refreshing old movie memories.

Between Santa Barbara and the megalopolis to the southeast is an inhospitable terrain that defies development: the Rincon. It is the cherished barrier against "Los Angelization." The Santa Ynez Mountains rim Santa Barbara on the north. They are the demarcation between Central and Southern California weather zones. These two natural bastions are nature's legacy to a city that is unique and beautiful. Santa Barbara is lucky but not immune. Its quality of life is threatened. Traffic is congesting, housing is being doubled-up and tripled-up, the water supply is over-committed. Santa Barbara and similar choice locales throughout the country and about the globe are stressed by population pressures. Paradise has its optimum limits; bursting them, we yearn for how it used to be—and is no more.

From Santa Barbara heading toward Hearst Castle, take the San Marcos Pass into the Santa Ynez Valley. This pristine picture postcard place is safe from urbanization—for the moment. This Valley is a horse haven, its theme set in bronze with equine statuary at Federico's and the Holiday Inn west of Solvang. The life-size rearing horses and raging bull are magnificent, and for what these sculptures cost, one could have bought all of Buellton when I first saw it.

The valley sites two more missions. La Purisima is at Lompoc. In spring and early summer it has, for a backdrop, a thousand acres of flowers in bloom, the fringe benefit of a flower-seed industry. Solvang has the Santa Ines mission, but you may not even look for it because you're bound to get caught up in shopping. This community is a Danish delight! An architectural transplant from Europe in miniature. The amazing thing is it was achieved without CCR's or zoning. Sometimes things just happen—like Solvang.

Departing this Danish smorgasbord is like pulling teeth. But just an hour's drive north is another memory-maker. Oh-my-oh-my!

210

The Courthouse of Santa Barbara

A crusader, Charles Fletcher Lummis, who was dedicated to saving Santa Fe and the Romance of the Missions, once delivered a sermon which roused the civic blood pressure of Santa Barbara. It was two years before the earthquake. The following extract speaks a timely admonition to this city and this state, threatened as they are with growth strangulation:

" . . . do you dream that anybody will ever build in Santa Barbara another building that will mean so much to Santa Barbara and to the world as the gray Old Mission? No one ever will.

American enterprise is all-powerful. It can tame wilderness, level mountains, lead rivers by the nose 300 miles, drag heat and light and power from the inwards of the earth. It can turn a hamlet into a Los Angeles in 30 years. It can build a Chicago—it could build a hundred Chicagos. But ALL THE BRAINS, ALL THE BRAWN, ALL THE MONEY IN AMERICA CANNOT BUILD A VENERABLE FRANCISCAN MISSION, NOR THE TOMB OF JUNIPERO SERRA.

Furthermore, no matter what fine monuments we do build, they will never have the same Romance, even with the coming centuries—for reasons obvious to the historian. There can no more be again a Father Junipero than there could be a Richard Lion-Heart. The Heroic, the Chivalric, the Apostolic ages are gone forever. There will never be another Parthenon, another Sphinx, another Mission . . . "

Photo courtesy of The Madonna Inn, San Luis Obispo, California

35

Madonna Inn

Of all the attractions in this book, were I allowed but a single one in the entire U.S.A., the eliminations would be difficult, even painful, but my choice would be the HEARST CASTLE. It is the ultimate ego-creation. And there is more. Its location atop a mountain overlooking the blue Pacific is breathtaking. Still more: the only way to get there is along the Big Sur Highway (California Highway One) which has to be the top scenic drive experience on this continent. And one more reason: I cannot reach the Big Sur Highway without first coming to an exit marked "Madonna Road." I never pass it by.

What a duo! Hearst Castle, the supreme extravagance that transplanted European art and architecture to the Pacific shores, and, an easy hour's drive south, the Madonna Inn, a creation transplanted from nowhere—except the audacious imagination of a zany and rich pair of small-town innkeepers, Alex and Phyllis Madonna.

Before you arrive you are conditioned for *pink*—passionate pink! Billboards, approaching from either direction on Highway 101, are pink, the gas station pumps, lampposts, trash cans, the public telephone—all pink. And the dining room is breathtaking, blushing, sensuous, seductive—in PINK!

If ever a hostelry was built just for the hell of it, it's the Madonna Inn at San Luis Obispo. This overnightery has 110 rooms, all different and all off-the-wall! I won't try to classify the architecture. It has all, it has none. It is rock-hound Flintstone; it is giddy colonial; it is Li'l Abner rustic; it is Hearst Castle leftover. It is pure MADONNA.

A wedding night at this place is the frosting on the cake. So many "just-marrieds" stake it out that phone reservations for weekending are nearly impossible.

Of all your travels in the USA, this place will be the most difficult to describe to your friends left behind, so I'll help with a one-liner: It is the Madonna-Monument-to-magnificent-madness. And a tribute to what an ingenious small-town couple did without an architect, designer or decorator. It would be a foolish person who tried to match it or compete with it.

Alexander Madonna was born into a ranching, dairying family north of San Luis Obispo in 1919, and attended a one-room school. The ranch was probably his best teacher. Married at thirty to Phyllis Boyd, they were to have four children. Just your solid American rural family. No education, no lineage to suggest an explosion of flair.

How did this creative splurge emerge? What started in 1935 when a sixteen-year-old school kid borrowed thirty dollars to buy a Model T truck, became a construction company with a thousand pieces of equipment—some still sitting on the "Ranch" beside the Inn.

You may ask "from whence came the money for all of this?" You were driving on it as you travelled the State. When California went freeway-crazy, Madonna was waiting with his infant constructioncompany. He started at the bottom; freeways catapulted him to the top. He and his wife plowed a lot of their money into their highway stop along 101. Once they started in 1958, they've never stopped. The Madonna family defied all the rules and built a monument. And it is located right where it belongs: on the Madonna home turf—San Luis Obispo, a not-too-large California coastal city with a well-behaved labor pool from Cal Poly.

Most travelers have a priority at a highway stop, and it isn't food. A frequently-heard anecdote from this showplace is of having ogled the "other restroom" (while a companion guards the door) . . . "you've gotta see this restroom."

When we Southern Californians host visitors from the north, a common greeting is, "Surely, you *did* stop at the Madonna Inn." Occasionally one *didn't*. We send them back.

At first encounter by the road-weary, the main dining area seems too fairylandish to enter--which is no problem because the food is just as tasty in the . . . What shall I call it? . . . not coffee shop? Not cafe? No label fits. Carvings—copper—carpet—color . . . see for yourself. And when you do, note at the rear of the room two booths separated by a fireplace. Overhead is a massive beam that appears to be leather, not fir, and you sense it belongs to the history of the Inn. The walls of the booths are covered with plaques and frames and newspaper headlines and awards as "man of the (everything!)." On the walls, among the trophies, is a pick and shovel—no doubt constant reminders that blisters and elbow-grease belong in this family's archives. Within this alcove the Madonna family often dines. This is the quality-control center, a view to what matters most, happy customers.

Reservations are oftentimes tight, but there's a way. I'll share a secret . . . standby works amazingly well. The desk clerk once told me I was forty-six. My place down the waiting list? (Or did she think it was my age?) Hopeless? There's *always* hope. Three P.M. is the cut-off when "no-shows" and "no deposits" get scratched. Surprise!

My wife and I were checked into one of Madonna's caveman rooms. It had a bathroom which brought back memories of crawling over rocks to reach a waterfall. We cuddled in a cave, chuckling with delight. Plush, garish and pinked-out.

That evening, out in the parking area, there were dozens of cars with "just married" signs, and in the dining room, starry-eyed youngster-couples braved the dance floor, struggling with orchestra music that turned their parents on.

This night we dance with the honeymooners. Tomorrow we play with the movie stars at the Enchanted Castle.

Photo by J. Blades, courtesy of Hearst San Simeon State Hist. Monumen

36

Hearst Castle
La Cuesta Encantada

STOP THE CAR! As one drives north on Highway One toward Big Sur, leaving the scented pine forest about Cambria and emerging into open grasslands and scattered oak groves that cover the Santa Lucia Mountain slopes, a three-dimensional panorama tugs for attention. First, one searches the ocean bluffs along which the flat highway weaves. The restless surf crashing against the jagged coast is a never-ending fascination, but invariably your gaze sweeps the mountains, and there it is! Miles away, dominating a mountain pedestal—a CAMEO? Up closer, could it be a MURAL? You strain your eyes for detail.

Your first sighting of La Cuesta Encantada is of an apparition. Silent. Mysterious. Untouchable. It is "The Enchanted Hill," a matchless work of art sculptured atop the mountain by a MAN! And a WOMAN! The Man: giant of stature, purse and inspiration; the Woman: diminutive of body, but immense of talent, strong of will, inexhaustible of energy. William Randolph Hearst's "ranch house," Julia Morgan's commission. It is the Western Hemisphere's contest entry for human superlative. Hanging Gardens of Babylon, Granada, Istanbul, Versailles, Castles on the Rhine—also winners, but this is the blue ribbon. The inspirations of the Renaissance, a European travel itinerary brought to easy reach of a single interlude on American shores!

This romantic mirage on the mountain where it overlooks a vast domain is a visual statement that not all men (and women) are born equal. It is a demonstration of what genius in the genes can do—especially when embodied in an only son of a doting mother who was funded by the Homestake, the Comstock, the Anaconda, and a bevy of other money-gushing mining resources.

"STOP THE CAR, Jeanne! I need to reminisce." You see, shortly after I was born, Hearst contacted the promising young architect to lay out an upgrade for his tent camp on San Simeon ranch. He moved into his uncompleted home about the same time my family moved into a much more modest one a few miles south, in Santa Maria. We were close enough to San Simeon to know about the trainloads and boatloads of material bound for the biggest private construction project in California. Many of the local folks worked there, camping through the week and returning weekends to tell exaggerated tales that defied belief.

Even a second-grader knew from the table chatter that at Hearst's house one did not eat in the kitchen, the back door screen did not bang, and the stuff which overflowed *his* garage was art, not junk. We would never know the details, but there at the end of the road was a magic land, a world apart.

"Can we go see it?" I pleaded with my father.

"Sure—soon as you get famous or know how to lay tile," teased my sister who had been to the Emerald City of Oz, with Dorothy.

"Sinful! They should have given the money to the poor . . . " admonished my mother, who would then quote "poor" from the scriptures.

Thirty-five years after table-talk-time at Santa Maria, and before that first glimpse, much happened to Hearst's mountaintop and the world. Lindbergh shrank the Atlantic and dined at the "Castle," the Depression nearly destroyed the country (and Hearst), WWII changed the world (and resuscitated Hearst's finances), Korea was over and the King was gone—laid to rest in the Hearst mausoleum at Colma, south of San Francisco.

Even as I gazed and reminisced beside the road, the Hearst family was completing a transfer of La Cuesta Encantada to the State. And architect Julia Morgan lay dying. A year later, in 1958, it would be a state historical monument, and busloads of visitors would snake six miles up the mountain to the 1600-foot-high crest. They would unload starry-eyed, and guides would try to explain the place to them.

Since it opened to the public, over twenty million visitors have been challenged to digest this matchless creation. How many of the visitors, including myself, can grasp what we view? Very few. What most do know is that they are overwhelmed. Like classroom children, we are ushered from marvel to marvel . . . we gaze and stare.

In one such group, a voice out of his fog asked the guide, "Why doesn't the state finish it?" A state bureacracy finish this masterpiece? Ludicrous! Who would be qualified? If Hearst and architect Morgan still lived and had the money, in all these intervening years the work would have progressed, but would never be finished. If Gutzon Borglum were still living, the carving at Mount Rushmore would still be chewing away at the mountain. Michelangelo would find another ceiling, and another. Great artists never finish.

George Hearst gave his son the San Francisco Examiner in 1887—because William wanted it—and a career was born. Hail to the media czar of the next century. He acquired newspapers, radio stations and movie studios. Half the nation was reading Hearst-slanted news, while the other half was watching his film epics. His influence was immense, as was his ego. He was elected to Congress for two terms (1902-1906), twice was defeated for Mayor of New York, and once was defeated for Governor of the state. In 1908 he made a presidential bid. If he couldn't be master of the White House, he could be Mogul of his mountain, a domain that stretched as far as his eye could see. So in 1919, he enlisted the help of his mother's protege-architect, Julia Morgan. She had talent to match Hearst's prodigious energy. She would design his palace to house the shiploads of European art he was collecting. It was a lifetime commitment, and would be going on yet had the two not died.

Hearst's biographies are plentiful. The easiest to read is right in the visitor's center, an engrossing visual walk through the man's life and works. What you see at San Simeon is hard to grasp, so take advantage of this assist. Don't begrudge the hour it might take. W.R. Hearst and Julia Morgan spent twenty-eight years . . . and spent and spent and spent!

Your trip to the top is by park-operated bus. A fifteen-minute ride. Exercise, if you need it, will come soon.

There are four separate tours. I have taken them all. "Come on, memory—describe it for your readers."

Well, on the trip up the mountain, we pass through thousands of acres where herds of imported wild animals once grazed. Now there are some zebra mingled with lots of cattle.

After some introductory background, our guide leads us to the esplanade. It is a colorful walkway that joins the three distinctive guest houses to Casa Grande. Today our group is delayed while young William Hearst, Jr. is being instructed in the game of cricket. I remark that it's a silly game—baseball makes more sense. The instructor turns around to scold me, and I apologize. I would never purposely offend David Niven, and now I have missed some important statuary on the terrace.

We then come to the Neptune Terrace. The design is exquisite, the view breathtaking. Between two Grecian columns, Gutzon Borglum is arguing with Louella Parsons. I try to eavesdrop, and I miss some of the guide's commentary.

The Neptune Pool you won't believe. There's a temple and statue of the god of the sea. Greta Garbo was splashing water in John Gilbert's face, and it was very distracting.

The guide took us into the Assembly room. It has an Italian Renaissance ceiling, tapestries, lots of carvings; it's like a hotel lobby. Albert Einstein was studying a carving, Venus of Canova, I learned. We slipped on past lest we intrude on some profound equation in formulation.

The refectory has the longest dining table I have ever seen. There was a small group having lunch. Hearst was debating England's faults with Winston Churchill and Calvin Coolidge was listening in. Marion Davies, across the table, chided the president to support W.R., but Cal remained silent. We tiptoed out.

The library was impressive. Ceiling from a castle in Aragon, a shelf beneath lined with Greek pottery. A friendly room with lots of rare books. George Bernard Shaw was leafing through some worn volumes. Looking for material for a play, no doubt. I didn't linger.

There's a cozy theater, austere compared to what we've been seeing. Louis Mayer and Irving Thalberg were watching a screening.

It grabbed me, but the guide told us we must move on. Said we could see it at the Orpheum in a few months.

The Roman Pool had me speechless. A million dollars and Julia Morgan's inspiration kept all the surplus Italian-American tile-layers employed for four years. If I could only take a dip to tell my grandchildren about, it would be a lasting thrill—but Norma Shearer and Rudolph Valentino were cavorting in the water and I was too shy to ask if I might join them.

We checked out the tennis courts. Tennis was W.R.'s favorite sport. It's mine, too. A mixed doubles match was in progress. Helen Wills and Bill Tilden were paired off against Alice Marble and Fred Perry. What a lucky chance encounter. They're out of my league, I know.

Plantings are profuse, gardens everywhere. In a bed of roses is the sculpture of Europa astride a bull. A pathetic-looking little guy was trying to drape his wrinkled coat around the nude. The guide told him not to touch the art. "Just clowning," was Chaplin's retort as he brushed both palms on his rumpled pants and ambled off.

Preservation of the art and structures is a major concern for the park department. Since 1984, curators have been added to the staff to concentrate on restoration, and in the visitor center is an area for viewing this type of crafting.

The return down the mountain is a long, winding ride. Gives the visitor lots of time to cogitate. There is so much to file away in the memory, so much emotion to vent. It's been a day in a strange and foreign culture.

I'm smiling. I've been to the inner sanctum. At long last I was able to stand beside the Neptune Pool. And I speculate: How many in my busload realize theirs was a privilege which Hearst's own father, who made the money, and Phoebe Apperson, his mother who nurtured the inspiration, could never savor? The two people who provided the genes and wealth for their progeny never knew the ecstasy. But we know.

"Hello—People in this bus! Ask yourself, When in your wildest imagination did you ever dream of a day such as this? Let us conclude this experience by extolling some truly amazing people."

First, a salute to George Hearst (1820-1891), a common man from Missouri who went west in 1850 with the gold fever. He sought a better life—he over-achieved a thousand-fold.

Our respects to the nineteen-year-old he married in June of '62 . . . the girl next door, 22 years his junior, a school teacher with a yen for culture. She bore one son, instilled him with lofty ambitions, inherited a vast fortune which allowed her to become one of the most generous, hard-working, dedicated women philanthropists of all time. Phoebe Apperson Hearst (1842-1919) earned her place in the hall of fame.

Three more unique women embellished William Randolph's world: Millicent Willson Hearst, the New York lady who was his wife for life and mother of five sons, matron of the Sands Point, Long Island estate, and philanthropist; Marion Davies—actress, companion, court jester and accessory; and Julia Morgan, the artist-architect-engineer who translated Hearst's vision-whimsy-extravagance into tangible beauty. California is dotted with her Hearst assignments. She is the most renowned woman architect of our age.

Five men, the sons of William Randolph and Millicent Willson Hearst, are the benefactors who determined that La Cuesta Encantada should be given to the public. Undoubtedly, W.R. knew and intended that there could be no other ultimate destiny. Yet the decision was made by George, William Jr., John, Randolph and David Hearst. "Thank you" sounds so feeble. Someone come forth with an adequate word.

"Attention everyone! Just think. Until 1958, only the King's ministers and courtiers knew the exhilaration we have experienced. Now we have joined their exclusive company. And even though we must descend to a mundane world, we do have a shared bond with Julia Morgan and W.R. Hearst, and those illustrious guests who have travelled this roadway. We've all savored the San Simeon Memorial; we've all been to the mountain top!"

Epilogue

"But, Where Is *Your* Favorite?"

I have an apology. This grouping is incomplete. Great cities have been by-passed, and equally deserving attractions omitted. The trail keeps unfolding, even as this book goes to press. Your favorite may be awaiting the sequel.

Quizzical readers may ask why handiworks of nature are not included. Natural wonders are awe-inspiring and the travel favorites of millions, especially children. Fortunately, nature has ample advocacy through our numerous park systems.

I narrowed my selections to those which met the following criteria: the uniquely distinctive creation of a private luminary, aged enough to deserve a place in the hall of fame, open to the public, of historic or social significance, and/or architectural landmarks.

The book to follow will be broader, and will include religious shrines and sports meccas. It will focus on great cities crowded out of this first book, including Atlanta, Chicago, Cleveland, Dallas-Fort Worth, Kansas City, Nashville (including my interview with the goddess Athena), the Twin Cities and points south and west. My criteria may bend to reach Hull/Ottawa for the Museum of Civilization . . . and from there I have a springboard to the Grand Hotel on Mackinac Island

It's a rainbow without end.

Hal Thornton

Disclaimer: The information provided is intended as a convenience to the reader. The traveller should anticipate the passage of time will cause changes in phone numbers, mailing addresses, street designations, hours of admittance, charges for admission, etc. Where the term "tax deductible" appears, it means deductible to the extent allowed by law. The author has attempted to give information that is applicable for 1990. Changes are inevitable. A prudent reader will understand the need for timely verification, especially as to driving directions. The information is arranged by chapter.

2   WHITEHALL   Cocoanut Row, Box 969
 (407) 655-2833   Palm Beach, FL 33480

Hours: 10-5 Tuesday-Saturday; 12-5 Sunday; closed Monday, Christmas and New Year's Day. *Directions*: From I-95 or Sunshine Parkway or U.S. 1, go east on Okeechobee Blvd., cross Lake Worth, turn left at Cocoanut Row. Small admission charge. Tax-deductible membership.

2   THE BREAKERS HOTEL   One South County Road
 Reservations: (800) 833-3141   Palm Beach, FL 33480
 (407) 659-8440

Directions: Located in the center of Palm Beach, six miles from Palm Beach International Airport, 65 miles north of Miami. From I-95 or Florida's turnpike, exit West Palm Beach/Okeechobee Blvd., drive east to South County Road, then north one mile to the hotel.

3   VIZCAYA   3251 South Miami Avenue
 (305) 579-2708   Miami, FL 33129

Hours: 9:30-5 daily; closed Christmas. Group tours may be scheduled in advance—call (305) 579-2808. Cafe on the premises. Admission charge $8 (1990). Vizcaya Foundation welcomes tax-deductible donations. *Directions*: Southbound on I-95, use exit 1 and watch for signs. Vizcaya is about one-half mile south of the Rickenbacker Causeway entrance. It's tricky, so be alert.

4   THE BILTMORE HOTEL   1200 Anastasia Avenue
 Reserv: (800) 445-2586   Coral Gables, FL 33134
 (305) 445-1926

Directions: Driving from Vizcaya: U.S. 1 south to Bird Road, turn right after approximately half a mile, onto Grenada. At first four-way stop, the hotel is on the left.

5   RINGLING MUSEUM OF ART   5401 Bayshore Road
     AND CIRCUS GALLERIES   Sarasota, FL 34243
     (813) 355-5101

Hours: 10-6 daily; closed major holidays. Restaurant on premises; picnic area. Nominal admission fee. Tax-deductible membership: Ringling Museum. Recommended reading: The John and Mabel Ringling Museum of Art, by Patricia Ringling Buck; available at museum shops. *Directions*: Driving south on U.S. 41 from St. Petersburg/Tampa, exit right at sign just past the Sarasota airport.
For scheduling of the Baraboo Museum's train and Milwaukee parade, contact Great Circus Parade Office, 1421 N. Water Street, Milwaukee, Wisconsin 53202. Circus World Museum, Baraboo, Wisconsin 608-356-8341

6   JEKYLL ISLAND and   Visitors Bureau
     JEKYLL ISLAND CLUB HOTEL   P.O. Box 3186
                              Jekyll Island, GA 31520
   Hotel Reservations: (800) 333-3333   Visitor Info: (800) 841-6586

Hours: Tours: meet at Orientation Center for tram rides through the historic district; 10-2 during winter; 10-4 during summer. Numerous modern restaurants and motels. The Jekyll Island Museum Association helps fund the "Historic District" and welcomes tax-deductible contributions; send to 375 Riverview Drive, Jekyll Island, Georgia 31520. *Directions*: Exit I-95 to Brunswick (via U.S. 17 coastal highway). Take Jekyll Island Causeway (south of the Brunswick drawbridge). Pick up a map at the Welcome Center before reaching the island.

6   THE CLOISTER Resort   Sea Island, GA 31561
     (800) SEA-ISLA

Only registered guests are admitted to dining and refreshment services. For midday lunching, the Cloister golf course at south end of St. Simons is not restricted. Recommended reading: *This Happy Isle* by Harold H. Martin, published by Sea Island Company. *Directions*: Take causeway east from Brunswick, to St. Simons Island and turn left at Sea Island Road. The signs are subtle, so stop and inquire if necessary.

6   THE KING AND PRINCE RESORT   P.O. Box 798
     (800) 342-0212   St. Simons Island, GA 31522

Directions: Take causeway east from Brunswick to St. Simons Island, to Kings Way, then Ocean Blvd.

7   THE BILTMORE ESTATE   One North Pack Square
    (800) 543-2961   Asheville, NC 28801
Hours: 9-5 daily (ticket office); closed major holidays. Restaurants on the grounds.
Admission: $19.00 (1990); group rates available. Privately owned by Vanderbilt
heirs. Recommended reading: The Magnificent Builders, by Joseph J. Thorndike,
Jr., published by American Heritage Publishing Company; Biltmore Estate, by the
Biltmore Company. *Directions*: Exit from I-40. Signs exist but are somewhat
confusing. Location is south edge of Asheville—a city with a spaghetti-like highway
grid. For directions here, get a second opinion (a third would be even better).

8   GROVE PARK INN   290 Macon Avenue
    (800) 438-5800   Asheville, NC 28804
Directions: I-240 to Charlotte St. exit (5B). Go north on Charlotte one-half mile.
Turn right on Macon Ave., which will lead you to the hotel.

9   MONTICELLO   P.O. Box 316
    (804) 295-2657   Charlottesville, VA 22902
Hours 9-4:30 daily. Admission $7 (1990). (Your change may include a crisp
$2 bill bearing Jefferson's face.) Tax-deductible contributions to Thomas Jefferson
Memorial Foundation are welcome and needed. (Be generous Jefferson did not
leave an endowment.) *Directions*: Four miles southeast of Charlottesville. From
I-64 at Charlottesville, take Highway 20 South, left on Route 53.

9   The HOMESTEAD Resort   Hot Springs, VA 24445
    (800) 336-5771   (703) 839-5500
Directions: Off Highway 220. Exit is marked.

9   The GREENBRIER Resort   White Sulphur Springs, West VA 24986
    (800) 624-6070   (304) 536-1110
Directions: Off I-64. Exit is marked. Recommended reading: *The History of the
Greenbrier*, by Dr. Robert S. Conte (presently staff historian), available at the
Greenbrier gift shop.

10 LONGWOOD GARDENS   P.O. Box 501
    (215) 388-6741   Kennett Square, PA 19348
Hours: Conservatory, Winter 9-5; Spring 10-5; Outside garden, 9-6. Restaurant
is open March to December. Admission $8 adults, $2 children (1990).
Directions: Make local inquiry for everything in Chapter 10. Brandywine area, 30
miles southwest of Philadelphia, 12 miles northwest of Wilmington between Ken-
nett Square and Chadds Ford. Parking access from Longwood Road near junction
of Route 52 and U.S. 1. Easy to get lost.

10 NEMOURS MANSION & GARDENS   P.O. Box 109
    (302) 651-6912   Wilmington, DE 19899
Visitors must be 16 or older. *Hours*: Reservation office open 8:30-4:30 Monday-Friday; two-hour tours at 9, 11, 1 and 3, Tuesday-Saturday. Food service available nearby at the Alfred I. duPont Institute. *Directions*: If using I-95 to Wilmington: exit 8 North (Concord Pike Route 202). Go two traffic lights to Route 141 and turn left. Go two traffic lights to Rockland Road and turn left. Follow to end of stone wall and turn right. Make an immediate right. Reception Center is the pink and glass building located in the parking lot of the medical Institute.

10 WINTERTHUR   Winterthur, DE 19735
    (800) 448-3883
Hours: 9-5 Tuesday-Saturday; 12-5 Sunday. Admission charge depends on selection of tour. There is a garden tram. Garden cafeteria on premises. Tax-deductible membership: Winterthur Guild. Directions: Located 30 miles southwest of Philadelphia, 5 miles south of Route 1 and Pennsylvania state line. From I-95, exit 7 (Delaware Avenue) to Route 52; continue approximately six miles, exit on right.

10 HOTEL DuPONT   11th & Market Street
    (800) 441-9019   Wilmington, DE 19899
    (800) 323-7500   (302) 594-3100

11 EMPIRE STATE BUILDING   Fifth Avenue at 34th St.
    (212) 736-3100   New York, NY 10118
Hours: 9:30-midnight daily and holidays (tickets sold until 11:30 p.m.). Recommended reading: *The Empire State Building*, by Philip Van Doren Stern, published by Empire State Building, Helmsley Spear, Inc.; *The Empire State Building Book*, by Jonathan Goldman.

12 COLONIAL WILLIAMSBURG   P.O. Box C
    Visitor Center: (804) 229-1000   Williamsburg, VA 23187
    Williambsurg Inn: 1- 800 - HISTORY
Directions: Approx. one hour east of Richmond, I-64 East, exit 56, follow green sign to Visitor Center. $17 adult; $9 child (basic ticket). Foundation operated and supported.

12 THE CLOISTERS Museum   Fort Tryon Park
       (212) 923-3700   New York, NY 10040
Hours: 9:30-5:15 Tuesday-Sunday. Closed Monday and major holidays. *Directions*: Subway—(IND) 8th Avenue A Train to 190th Street (Overlook Terrace), exit by elevator, then take #4 bus or walk through Fort Tryon Park to the museum; Bus—Madison Avenue Bus #4 to "Fort Tryon Park"; Car—from Manhattan, take Henry Hudson Parkway north to the first exit after the George Washington Bridge.

13 NEWPORT MANSIONS   118 Mill Street
       The Preserv. Soc. of Newport   Newport, RI 02840
       (401) 847-1000
Hours: 10-5 daily. *Directions*: Highway 138 or 138A, goes through the center of Newport Village to Bellevue Avenue. Signs abound.

13 Admirals B&B   Write: 8 Fair Street
       (800) 343-2863   Newport, RI 02840

14 ISABELLA STEWART GARDNER MUSEUM 2 Palace Road
       (617) 566-1401   280 The Fenway
                                             Boston, MA 02115
Hours: 12-5 daily; closed Monday and national holidays. Cafe on premises. Nominal admission; museum has membership and welcomes tax-deductible support. *Directions*: From downtown Boston, go southwest on Huntington Avenue to Louis Prang Street. Turn right to Fenway; museum is on the left. Park on street or across at Museum of Fine Arts (which you'll wish to see). Better—don't drive.

15 SHELBURNE MUSEUM   Route 7
       Recording: (802) 985-3344   Shelburne, VT 05482
       Admin. Offices: (802) 985-3346
Hours: 9-5 daily. Food service on premises. $8 admission (1990). Tax-deductible contributions are welcome and needed. Recommended reading: *A Pictorial History of Shelburne Museum*, available in museum shop; *An American Sampler: Folk Art from the Shelburne Museum*, catalog available in museum shop. *Directions*: Seven miles south of Burlington, Vermont, on Route 7. Approximately 15 minutes from Burlington Int'l Airport.

15   SHELBURNE HOUSE and FARMS   Shelburne, VT 05482
(802) 985-8498 (late May to mid-Oct.)
(802) 985-8686 (mid-Oct. to late May)

Hours: Tours daily, May 27 through October 15; inquire for time. Shelburne Farms Resources is an independent, non-profit, educational organization. *Directions*: Westbound from Interstate 89, exit 13; take Route 7 south four miles to traffic light, turn right onto Bay Road. From the south on Route 7, turn left at traffic light in the center of Shelburne. Drive 1.6 miles to the entrance of Shelburne Farms, proceed through the stone gate and follow signs (two miles) to Shelburne House.

16   FRANKLIN D. ROOSEVELT
Home, Grave and Memorabilia

National Park Service
259 Albany Post Road
Hyde Park, NY 12538

Nominal entrance fee. Golden Age Pass admits free. *Directions*: about five miles north of Poughkeepsie on Highway 9.

17   VANDERBILT MANSION

National Park Service
Hyde Park, NY 12538

Hours: 9-5 daily; closed Christmas and New Year's Day (Visitors Center may be closed part of the winter). Nominal entrance fee. Golden Age Pass admits free. *Directions*: about six miles north of Poughkeepsie, on U.S. 9.

18   HERSHEY SCHOOL & FOUNDERS HALL   400 W. Hersheypark Drive
Information Center   Hershey, PA 17033
Phone: (800) HERSHEY

Hours: Founders Hall open 9-4 Monday-Friday, 10-5 Saturday-Sunday. *Directions*: The Hershey conglomerate is located just off Interstates 81, 83 and 76, a short distance east of Harrisburg, Pennsylvania.

18   HOTEL HERSHEY
(717) 533-2171

P.O. Box BB
Hershey, PA 17033

Dress code for dining room (inquire). *Directions*: Same as above. Complimentary transportation from Harrisburg Int'l Airport and Amtrak Station.

19   THE CARNEGIE
(412) 622-3315

4400 Forbes Avenue
Pittsburgh, PA 15213

Hours: 10-5 Tuesday-Friday, 1-5 Sunday; closed Monday and holidays. Dining area (table service) and cafeteria on premises. Nominal admission. For information about membership in The Carnegie, call (412) 622-3313. Directions: In the heart of Pittsburgh University area (Oakland); ten-minute bus ride from downtown.

19 HEINZ HALL   600 Penn Avenue
    (412) 392-4800   Pittsburgh, PA 15222
Open for special events as scheduled.

19 THE WESTIN WILLIAM PENN HOTEL   530 William Penn Place
    (800) 228-3000   Pittsburgh, PA 15219

20 STAN HYWET HALL   714 North Portage Path
    (216) 836-5533   Akron, OH 44303
Hours: 10-4 Tuesday-Saturday, 1-4 Sunday; closed Monday and major holidays.
Directions: Northwest of the city. Inquire for directions when approaching Akron.

20 QUAKER SQUARE HILTON HOTEL   135 S. Broadway
    1 - 800 - HILTONS   Akron, OH 44308
    (216) 253-5970

21 GREENFIELD VILLAGE and FORD MUSEUM   Mailing address:
    20900 Oakwood Blvd., Dearborn   P.O. Box 1970
    (313) 271-1620   Dearborn, MI 44308
    (800) 338-0125 (From central and eastern states)
Hours: 9-5 daily; closed Thanksgiving and Christmas. Historical building interiors
are closed January through mid-March, and some buildings may not be accessible
at various times throughout the year. Restaurants and rides operate on a seasonal
basis. *Directions:* Northeast of Detroit Airport and two miles from Dearborn
Amtrak Station. From U.S. 12 or 94, exit to Oakwood. Clearly marked.

22 JEFFERSON NAT'L EXP. MEMORIAL   11 North 4th Street
    ST. LOUIS ARCH (314) 425-4465   St. Louis, MO 63102
Hours: Arch—8am-10pm summer; 9-6 winter; Old Courthouse—8-4:30 year-
round. Monument to a Dream, 35-minute movie shows every 45 minutes. Tram
to the top at 10-minute intervals (reservation system begins when waiting time
reaches approximately 30 minutes). Nominal entrance fee—Golden Age pass
admits free. *Directions:* Access by Interstates 70 and 55 and along Sullivan Blvd.
(riverfront). Parking garage at north end of the Arch grounds.

22 GRANT'S FARM   10501 Gravois Road
    Tour Reserv: (314) 843-1700   St. Louis, MO 63123
Hours: tour times hourly 9-3, Tuesday-Sunday in summer season; Thursday-
Sunday in fall season. Admission free, courtesy of Anheuser-Busch Company.
Directions: Gravois Road is State 30, southwest of the Arch, inside the circumfer-
ential expressway. Exit Grant Road.

22 MISSOURI BOTANICAL GARDEN   4344 Shaw Blvd.
    (314) 577-5100   St. Louis, MO 63110

Hours: 9-5 daily (winter); 9-8 daily Memorial Day through Labor Day; closed Christmas. *Directions*: Ten minutes west of the Arch via I-44. Inquire for best exit. Park off Shaw Blvd.

22 CATHEDRAL OF ST. LOUIS   4431 Lindell Blvd.
    (New Cathedral)   (at Newstead Ave.)
    (314) 533-2824   St. Louis, MO 63108

Hours: 7-6 daily; free tours Sunday at 1:00. *Directions*: Due west of the Arch, an easy cab ride. If driving, inquire for best street choices.

23 MOUNT RUSHMORE NAT'L MEM.   Superintendent, N.P.S. Box 268
    (605) 574-2523   Keystone, SD 57751

Hours: Visitors Center 8-5 in winter, 8am-10pm in summer. Food service available. Admission free. *Directions*: 25 miles southwest of Rapid City. From I-90 exit to U.S. 16/385. Ample signs.

  The Mount Rushmore National Memorial Society is a public-spirited support group that channels much-needed tax-deductible gifts to the preservation of this monument. Contact: Mount Rushmore Society, P.O. Box 1524, Rapid City, South Dakota 57709.

23 CRAZY HORSE   Avenue of the Chiefs
    (605) 673-4681   Crazy Horse, SD 57730-9998

Hours: Visitors Center, 7—dusk, daily, year-round. Food Service at Laughing Waters Restaurant (in season). A non-profit project for the Indians of North America, it has no governmental support. A nominal admission fee helps; a tax-deductible contribution helps more. *Directions*: Southwest of Rapid City. From I-90 exit to U.S. 16/385. 17 miles southwest of Mount Rushmore.

24 FAIRMONT HOTEL   Address: Atop Nob Hill
    Reserv: (800) 527-4727   San Francisco, CA 94106

Directions: Just drive to the top of Nob Hill, or catch Powell Street or California Street cable cars (discount for seniors).

25 EXPLORATORIUM   3601 Lyon Street
    (415) 561-0363   San Francisco, CA 94123

Hours: 10-9:30 Wednesday, 10-5 Thursday-Sunday; closed Monday and Tuesday. Directions: Located in the Palace of Fine Arts (Marina District) near the Bay, along the east edge of the Presidio. Take U.S. 101 (Lombard) or Marina Blvd. Inquire for best exit. If you miss the exit westbound, you may as well enjoy the Golden Gate Bridge.

26 PALACE OF THE LEGION OF HONOR   Lincoln Park
     deYOUNG MUSEUM and ASIAN ART MUSEUM   Golden Gate Park
     (415) 863-3330   San Francisco, CA

Hours: 10-5 Wednesday-Sunday; closed Monday and Tuesday. Admission $4, seniors $2 (save ticket—it's good for both museums). Dining 10-4 at de Young. *Directions*: deYoung museum is in Golden Gate Park between 8th and 10th Avenues. Several accesses include John Kennedy Drive. Cars are not allowed to park in Golden Gate Park on Sunday. Legion of Honor: Use 34th and Clement. Note Chapter 26 map.

27 MONTEREY BAY AQUARIUM   886 Cannery Row
     Public Info: (408) 648-4888   Monterey, CA 93940

Hours: 10-6 daily; closed Christmas. Admission charge. Inquire about membership program. Food service available. *Directions*: Exit Hwy 1 southbound at Del Monte, northbound at Munras. Follow signs to Cannery Row.

28 BALBOA PARK and SAN DIEGO ZOO   San Diego, CA 92101
     Park Info: (619) 236-5717   Zoo Info: (619) 234-3153

Hours: Zoo open 9-dusk daily; free Spreckels Organ concerts Sunday at 2 (except in February). Numerous food services available. This is a very big attraction--eight museums and a world-renowned zoo create lots of traffic. Preferably, have a route briefing before venturing forth. *Directions*: Located in central San Diego. Southbound on I-5, exit to 8-East and then 163-South, which leads to Park Blvd. Free parking.

29 HOTEL DEL CORONADO   1500 Orange Avenue
     (619) 522-8000   Coronado, CA 92118
     (800) 522-1200 in Calif.   (800) 522-3088 outside Calif.

Directions: I-5 exit to Coronado Bay Bridge.

30 SPRUCE GOOSE and HOTEL QUEEN MARY P.O. Box 8
     (213) 435-3511   Long Beach, CA 90801

Directions: Long Beach Freeway south to Harbor Scenic Drive to Pier J. If intending to register at the Queen Mary, the Hotel skywalk solves the access to the Spruce Goose. (Easier parking, too.)

31 THE HUNTINGTON LIBRARY   1151 Oxford Road
     (818) 405-2147   San Marino, CA 91108

Hours: 1-4:30 Tuesday-Sunday; closed Monday and major holidays. Sunday visitors are required to have advance parking reservations. Phone (818) 405-2100. *Directions*: Located south of Pasadena. From Foothill Freeway (210), exit at Sierra Madre Blvd. From Pasadena Freeway, exit east on California Blvd.

32   SAN SYLMAR (Merle Norman)   15180 Bledsoe Street
       (818) 367-2251   Sylmar, CA 91342

Advance reservations and escorted tours only. Phone or write and well in advance.
Ask for directions. Children under 13 not permitted. Dress code. Directions:
Northeast end of San Fernando Valley. Accessible from I-5, 405 and 210 (exit
Freeways Roxford). Use street parking. Odyssey Restaurant in Granada Hills:
(818) 366-2444.,

33   THE J. PAUL GETTY MUSEUM   Mailing address:
       17985 P.C.H., Malibu   Attn: Reservations
       (213) 459-8402   P.O. Box 2112
       (Info & parking reserv.)   Santa Monica, CA 90406

Hours: 10-5 Tuesday-Sunday; closed Monday and major holidays. Your car must
have a parking reservation. *Directions*: Entrance just north of Sunset on Pacific
Coast Highway. Use right (curb) lane and be alert—traffic is heavy and there's not
much warning. (The street entry is underwhelming.)

34   S.B. MISSION and COURTHOUSE   Santa Barbara, California

Hours: both open daily, year-round. Courthouse occupies the 1100 block of
Anacapa and/or Santa Barbara streets. Public parking (free as of 1990) across the
street on Anacapa. Mission is accessible from Laguna or Los Olivos Street (becomes Mission Canyon Road). *Directions*: Hwy 101 slices through Santa Barbara. A new freeway may be in place someday (Santa Barbarans are not sure) and
signs will change. For early 1990s, southbound on 101, exit east at Mission Street
for both of these attractions. Northbound on 101, exit Santa Barbara Street (someday, maybe, use Garden Street).

35   MADONNA INN   100 Madonna Road
       Reservations: (800) 543-9666   San Luis Obispo, CA 93401

U.S. 101 - exit Madonna Road (If you miss this one you're color-blind.)

36 HEARST STATE HISTORICAL MONUMENT   San Simeon,
                                               CA 93452

Reservation: Phone or write MISTIX
   (619) 452-5956 (customer service)
in Calif. (800) 444-PARK   P.O. Box 85705
outside Calif. (619) 452-1950   San Diego, CA 92138

Admission: (1990) $10 adult, $5 ages 6-12; children under 5 free if not occupying a bus seat. Reservations can be made up to eight weeks in advance or as late as the day of the tour. Walk-ins work if timing is right and depending on your choice of tour. Visa and MasterCard accepted. There are four separate tours, each about two hours, each some steps to climb. Directions: Northbound—Highway 1 from San Luis Obispo; southbound—Highway 101 to Paso Robles, then Highway 46 West to Highway 1 and north to the castle. Also Big Sur Highway south from Monterey-Carmel; a rewarding route, but can't be rushed.

Estimated driving time (as of 1990) from San Francisco: via U.S. 101 (245 miles)—6 hours; via Hwy 1 through Monterey/Carmel (205 miles)—6 hours plus. From Los Angeles via U.S. 101 and Highway 1 (250 miles)—6 hours minimum, depending on traffic. From San Luis Obispo (42 miles)—1 hour (plus pullover time to scan the shoreline).

DEFENSIVE STRATEGY: California, especially the coastal area, has more attractions and population than God intended. The stories you've heard about smog and freeway crawl are not rumors. Visitors do themselves (and California) a favor if they schedule away from Memorial Day to Labor Day. The weather will be better and the attractions less crowded in fall, winter and spring. Okay?

                                                H.L.T.

Index

About the Author

The author's life has been an odyssey. He has traveled extensively about the world—crossed Siberia by rail, hiked Alaskan tundra and portaged th Andes from Patagonia to Chile. In the U. S. he began his travels at age sixteen behind the wheel of a '26 Packard, criss-crossing the country as driver for his evangelist-father. He has chalked up all fifty states, lived in eleven of them, and **personally savored all the travel delights in this book.**

Thornton's favorite places are as diverse as Cordoba, Iguazzu Falls, Interlaken and Venice; the Opryland Hotel, San Juan Islands, Watkins Glen and Timberline Lodge.

His career has been that of a rolling stone. In Alaska, before statehood and money, he was a U. S. Commissioner, Jeep dealer, a bush pilot and commercial fisherman. With his wife he ran a repair garage, a roadhouse and a restaurant. After migrating to Puget Sound he dabbled in real estate, house-moving and even farming. Now in California, waiting for the big 'quake, he writes.

The author believes that a track record such as his qualifies him as an entrepreneur worthy of membership in that select Club of enterprisers with names that read like a turn-of-the-century Forbes 400: Carnegie, Flagler, Hershey, Ringling, Rockefeller, du Pont, Ford and Thornton (that's Harold L.) The author says these names have a common bond: Self-employed individualists, pioneers who challenged the status quo. They all struck it rich and left monuments as proof—except H. L. T.

Undaunted by a dozen or so pratfalls, Thornton explored an alternate tactic. He checked the tracks left by the winners and made a surprising discovery: Not one of them took immense wealth with him or her when they died.

A-h-h Ha! Then it must be around. It was easy tracking. These men—and women— left a part of their great fortunes highly visible. Unlocked! Right out in the open for everyone to share!

Andrew Carnegie declared that making lots of money is quite okay. However, before life's end the owner must share it with others. Carnegie's philosophy is called "The Gospel of Wealth." Thornton is willing to accept his share of the fruits of their enterprises. He calls his strategy "The Gospel of *Vicarious* Wealth."

Thornton says he is rolling in success—vicariously. The Club should admit him with an honorary category:

ENTREPRENEUR EMERITUS

LEVERAGE YOUR LEGACY
(a book in preparation)

ESTATE PLANNING should be a pleasure. So why isn't it? Do *wills, lawyers,* and *probate* induce confusion? Naturally! The thought of dying is a turn-off. "Living trust" isn't so soothing either. Why is it called *living* when we know it's about *dying*?

There is a better way. Hal Thornton has a simple strategy to make estate-transferal a shared experience—prolonged and meaningful. His concept is being detailed in a book now in preparation. It will show you how to make a legacy more enduring—and endearing.

The author has applied this method to his own estate planning. It is quite simple: it insures that those who have enjoyed being with you in *life* (spouse, children, cherished friends, and grandchildren) may continue this enjoyment after you are gone. They may retrace your travel delights; they may also claim vicarious wealth as advocated in *MONUMENTAL TREASURES.*

Your legacy to people you care for can be magnified by converting your money/property into experiences—good times shared just as though you were present.

Thornton provides an easy-to-follow guide for using a "special trustee" to avoid the pitfalls of an inflexible will or trust (the legal devices that all too often cause frustration, even litigation rather than joy and appreciation.) It applies whether your estate is $1,000 or $1,000,000.

If you find pleasure in great events and attractions like those featured in *MONUMENTAL TREASURES,* pass it on to your heirs. There is a way.

Use the order form (following page) to be notified when this new book is available. (Your lawyer should appreciate a copy, too.)

SHOPPING FOR A PRESENT?

You have just finished reading about 47 of America's great travel destinations (more to follow) and 14 of the nation's most impressive Hotels/Resorts. We hope this book will lead you to attractions you had previously overlooked or ignored. Perhaps you will want to share them with your friends.

YOU, too, may be a PHILANTHROPIST! Just as the movers and shakers, described on these pages, left their creations as a legacy to the viewer, you can be a *VICARIOUS* PHILANTHROPIST by bequesting the experience to your friends and family.

Make a gift of lasting memories and travel experiences to those you love. Give an awareness of these giants and their footprints from an earlier era. *MONUMENTAL TREASURES* brings the inspiration of those over-achievers from the past into your life, your living room.

With your order of five copies of *MONUMENTAL TREAS-URES* to give to your friends, we will mail a free copy of *LEVERAGE YOUR LEGACY* (see reverse) as soon as it is available from the printer.

- -

LEGACY PRESS
32 West Anapamu, Suite 284, Santa Barbara, CA 93101

Please send me ____ copy(s) of *Traveler's Guide to*
MONUMENTAL TREASURES

Enclosed is my check for $15.95 (per copy) plus $2 shipping.
(California residents add 6.5% sales tax)

____ Yes, I wish to receive information about
LEVERAGE YOUR LEGACY

_____
Name

_____
Address

_____
City, State, Zip